BY THE AUTO EDITORS OF CONSUMER GUIDE®

Great Cars
of the
SIXTIES

BEEKMAN
HOUSE

CONTENTS

Library of Congress Catalog Card Number:
ISBN 0-517-47924-9

This edition published by:
Beekman House
Distributed by Crown Publishers, Inc.
One Park Avenue
New York, New York 10016

Manufactured in the United States of America
10 9 8 7 6 5 4 3 2 1

Cover Design: Rich Franco

2

Photo Credits
Chevrolet Motor Division
Chrysler Historical Collection
Ford Motor Company
General Motors Design Staff
Pontiac Motor Division

Photography
John Apolinski
Terry Boyce
Douglas J. Mitchel
Dick Nesbitt

INTRODUCTION

Car enthusiasts remember the "Soaring Sixties" as the last full decade in which gas was cheap, the V-8 was undisputed king of the road, and new models appeared without fail in the fall. It was the decade that gave us the ponycar, the muscle car, and the personal-luxury car. It was the age of bucket seats and four-on-the-floor, "total performance" and "real fine 409s," the fastback and the "Scat Pack," cars named for animals, and street models aimed at the dragstrip. No doubt about it: the Sixties was the most exciting 10 years in postwar U.S. automotive history, and it's left us with a lot of happy memories.

And that brings up a problem with our title, *Great Cars of the Sixties*. Distinguishing the great from the not-

so-great is usually not a cut-and-dried task. But it gets really tricky when the subject is an emotional one—as automobiles most definitely are—and is examined with the inevitably altered perspective of 20 intervening years. Almost everyone has a favorite make or model, so any list of "great cars" is almost always subject to dispute.

Nevertheless, we think the 25 individual models profiled here represent the U.S. auto industry of the Sixties at its best. Because of limited space and other factors, we may have left out one or two models you might think should have been included. If that's the case, don't be offended: chances are you'll be seeing *More Great Cars of the Sixties*, in the very near future.

For now, feast your eyes on the bountiful beauties showcased in these pages, many professionally photographed especially for *Great Cars of the Sixties*. Significantly, almost all the cars pictured are fully restored examples, which is really no surprise: today there are more collectors devoted to American cars of this decade than any other. It's not hard to understand why. For one thing, Detroit abandoned the gimmickry and glitter of the Fifties for solid engineering innovations and tasteful styling. For another, the industry turned out a mind-boggling variety of cars in response to the needs of an increasingly sophisticated buying public, and it's because of this diversity that so many enthusiasts are attracted to Sixties machinery today. Moreover, the Sixties marked the end of what might be called America's "automotive adolescence," the last carefree years before the sober realities of safety and environmental concerns grew too great to ignore. Finally, these are the cars that most of America's postwar "baby boomers" grew up with during their own adolescence, which goes a long way in explaining the wide nostalgic appeal of Sixties cars in the Eighties.

Now a younger generation has discovered these cars, great and otherwise, joining the ranks of those like us who remember them when they were new. To all, we respectfully and joyfully dedicate *Great Cars of the Sixties*.

AMC AMX
1968-69

Gerald C. Meyers, former chairman and chief executive officer of American Motors, once called the two-seat AMX "the best-looking car, the most perfectly balanced car, that American Motors ever produced." AMC designer Richard Teague agrees that it was one of the prettiest designs to emerge from his studios, and collectors generally rate the AMX highly today.

Technically, the 1968 AMX was not "all-new." And given the limited budget that AMC had reserved for new products in the mid-1960s, it was remarkable that this sports car was built at all. If it hadn't been for the Javelin, AMC's 1968 entry in the pony-car arena, the AMX wouldn't have been born. The two-seater was actually a sectioned, short-wheelbase derivative of the Javelin, with a revised roofline and shorter rear quarter panels. Despite this close kinship with the garden-variety Javelin, the result was a modern classic.

The AMX was a true compact, with a trim 97-inch wheelbase, an overall length of 177.2 inches, and width of 71.6 inches. But the dimensions under that long, sleek hood were impressive. Three V-8s were offered, a standard 290-cid unit and optional 343 and 390 engines. All had four-barrel carburetors, but the new 390, rated at 315 horsepower, was the most popular choice. A special extra-cost performance package included "over-the-top" racing stripes, power disc brakes, red-line low-profile tires, higher-rate springs, "Twin-Grip" limited-slip differential, and heavy-duty engine cooling. Convenience options included power steering, power brakes, automatic transmission, tilt steering wheel, air conditioning, and tinted glass.

Standard AMX safety features included seat/shoulder belts, padded

This beautifully maintained example shows the clear relationship between the production AMX and the Javelin ponycar. Front-end sheetmetal and the basic instrument panel molding were shared. Cargo could be stowed in a shallow area behind the AMX's two buckets seats. (Owner: Joe Ward)

Top: "Big Bad" colors brightened up the '69 AMX, but styling changes were otherwise minimal. (Owner: Paul Gallo) Above: The sectioned structure and revised rear quarters gave the AMX ('68 shown) a unique look. (Owners: Bob and Jim Lojewski)

A prescient, confident American Motors even predicted collector interest in the two-seater: "We're only making 10,000 in 1968. We're even putting the production numbers on the dash for collectors who want to prove they got in on a great car fast." Sadly, sales were more limited than AMC anticipated. Production reached only 6725 for the first model year.

There were only minor changes for 1969. The "over-the-top" racing stripes were offered in more colors, and three new "Big Bad" hues gave the car a wild, new look. "Big Bad" production included 195 in blue, 284 in orange, and 283 in green. Even the bumpers were painted body color on these special editions. AMX exterior styling was unchanged, but interior trim was revised, a passenger grab bar was added, and shift quality on the four-speed manual transmission was improved. A leather-trimmed interior, in charcoal or saddle, was also new for '69. On June 29, an AMX served as the official pace car for the 47th annual Pike's Peak Hill Climb at Colorado Springs. Another honor came from the editors of *Industrial Design* magazine, who cited the AMX for "excellence of design." With all this and a 12-month model year, sales jumped to 8293 units.

Nineteen-seventy was the third and final season for the two-seat AMX. Despite new hood and grille styling, sales fell off and the car was killed at the end of the model year. The name did pop up occasionally in the Seventies on decal-emblazoned Javelins and Hornets, but these cars were far removed from the "classic" AMX.

Today, the AMX is remembered as one of the most exciting and collectible automobiles ever to come from American Motors. And the reasons aren't hard to find: exciting performance, fine styling, and the two-seat body style. Many collectors prefer the styling of the original 1968-69 car to the busier-looking 1970 model, but the earlier cars command no appreciable price premium. Values range from $500 to $700 for rough cars to $12,000 for a perfect example with the right options. Those options include the top-line 390 V-8, four-speed manual transmission, and the "Go" performance packages. The 390 engine was surprisingly popular with buyers, going into 4399 of the 6725 cars built for 68.

The AMX was introduced at the 1968 Chicago Auto Show to an enthusiastic public and motoring press. Finally, waxed the "buff book" editors, an AMC product that was spectacular, not just sensible. Tom McCahill, veteran car tester at *Mechanix Illustrated*, found the AMX "hairier than a Borneo gorilla and not the thing for Ma Peters' pie delivery route... Looks like it's doing 100 when parked." Alex Walordy told *Super Stock* readers, "You might as well stop polishing the '57 T-Bird, for American Motors has come up with something better. Their AMX is a tough machine, ready to handle all comers." The 390 AMX offered torrid performance in a hot-looking package. No wonder muscle-car fans were excited.

dash, four-way flashers, energy-absorbing steering column, and side marker lights. Unlike Corvette, its closest domestic competitor, AMX offered an all-steel, fully unitized body/chassis structure.

Other standards were reclining bucket seats, inflatable spare tire, 19-gallon gas tank, dual exhausts, four-speed transmission, tachometer, and a special suspension with rear traction bars.

BUICK RIVIERA 1963

After too many years of watching Ford's Thunderbirds go by, General Motors responded with a personal-luxury car of its own for 1963. Immediately hailed as an architectural milestone, the Buick Riviera set automotive style for the rest of the decade. GM also introduced a sharp new Chevrolet Corvette Sting Ray and a clean-lined Pontiac Grand Prix for '63, but Buick built the season's most acclaimed car.

The Riviera was inspired by a trip Bill Mitchell made to England in 1959. Mitchell, GM's top stylist, returned with the idea that any Thunderbird-fighter should be an elegant cross between a Rolls-Royce and a Ferrari. The Riviera was originally intended to be a Cadillac, and many of the early prototypes carried the LaSalle nameplate.

Oldsmobile and Pontiac also lobbied hard for it, but management decided that Buick needed an image-booster most of all. The Riviera name was a natural. Buick had been using it on hardtops since 1949, and it conveyed a sense of intrigue, exclusiveness, and upscale wealth.

Early proposals included a hardtop coupe, convertible, four-door hardtop, and even a four-door *phaeton*. Although the Thunderbird was available in both hardtop and convertible form, GM ultimately decided to offer the Riviera only as a hardtop coupe. In its final form, the car was a sensational blend of curves and razor-sharp edges. Frameless door glass, a minimum of chrome trim, and a low beltline gave it an airy elegance that set it apart in the luxury-car field.

If the styling was trend-setting, the Riviera's underpinnings were decidedly conventional and all-Buick. GM's time-tested cruciform frame was called into service to the dismay of safety advocates, who had been claiming for years that the design was unsafe in side impacts.

For its time, the Riviera was both relatively compact and relatively heavy, but Buick's 401-cid V-8 coupled with the venerable Turbine Drive automatic gave lively acceleration. *Motor Trend* magazine tested a Riviera with the optional 425-cid V-8 for its April 1963 issue, and liked it very much, the editors reporting a 0-60

Riviera bowed for '63 as Buick's answer to Ford's Thunderbird. (Owner: Dick Nesbitt)

mph time of 8.1 seconds, a top speed of 115 mph, and gas mileage between 11 and 15 mpg. *Car and Driver* also heaped on the praise: "Our opponents assert that the car is a big, heavy Buick and therefore completely undesirable for people who have enjoyed Jaguars, 300SLs, or even Corvettes. Actually, the Riviera is different from the other big Buicks, and it stands alone among American cars in providing a combination of luxury, performance and general road-worthiness that approaches Bentley Continental standards at less than half the price."

Even if the Riviera did wallow in the corners a bit, paying customers didn't mind. The V-8 was powerful, the Turbine Drive silky smooth, and the cabin was handsomely appointed even by traditional luxury-car standards. All-vinyl bucket seats were standard front

and rear. Interior colors were blue, silver, and sandalwood. A sharply hooded instrument panel provided a literal dash of class. Gauges were housed in two large pods directly in front of the driver, and the radio and climate controls were centrally located. A center console swept up to meet the dash, *a la* Thunderbird, but the effect was decidedly less "space age." The console contained the shift lever, a "smoking set" (ashtray and lighter), and rear floor courtesy lamps. For those who wanted the ultimate in luxury, a custom leather interior was available in blue, silver, white, red, black, and saddle.

With a base price of $4333, the Riviera was considered rather pricey in 1963, but its list of standard features was a long one. Although the base car was impressive enough, there was a

host of extras available. New for '63 was a steering wheel that could be tilted to one of seven different positions. Other options included cruise control, wire wheel covers, and an AM/FM radio.

Buick planned on building 40,000 of the elegant Rivieras for model year 1963, and they assembled exactly that many. The model was visually unchanged for '64, but a superior Super Turbine 400 (Turbo Hydra-Matic at other GM divisions) replaced the sometimes troublesome Turbine Drive. For '65 there were hidden headlights and revised trim all around. And then the bulk set it, making the first-generation Riviera the one to covet.

When it was new, copywriters called the '63 Riviera "Buick's bid for a great new international classic." And today, that's precisely what it is.

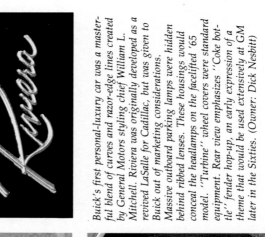

Buick's first personal-luxury car was a masterful blend of curves and razor-edge lines created by General Motors styling chief William L. Mitchell. Riviera was originally developed as a revived LaSalle for Cadillac, but was given to Buick out of marketing considerations.
Massive outboard parking lamps were hidden behind ribbed lenses. These housings would conceal the headlamps on the facelifted '65 model. "Turbine" wheel covers were standard equipment. Rear view emphasizes "Coke bottle" fender hop-up, an early expression of a theme that would be used extensively at GM later in the Sixties. (Owner: Dick Nesbitt)

CHEVROLET
BEL AIR 409 1962

The full-size 1961 Chevrolet was a winner everywhere but the race track. Chevy handily beat Ford on the sales charts with the clean new Impala, value-packed Bel Air, and thrifty Biscayne. But the division's top engine, the 348-cid V-8, could not beat the factory-prepared Fords and power-packed Mopars on the strip—or on the street.

After too many years on the sidelines, Chevy suddenly upped the performance ante in the spring of 1961 with a 360-bhp blockbuster measuring 409 cubic inches. This new V-8, based roughly on the venerable 348, was

showcased in a limited-production Impala dubbed Super Sport and pro-moted heavily in the "hot rod" press. With back-door assistance from head-quarters, it hit the strips at full tilt, winning every competition in sight and becoming a seldom-seen street legend in the process. The 409 was hot but hard to get. Only 142 were built for '61.

Amends were made for 1962. This season's 409 was good enough to sing about—which is exactly what a new surfing group called the Beach Boys did, immortalizing the big "Turbo-Fire" engine in a tribute that went to

the top of the record charts: "She's Real Fine, My 409."

The '62 409 was a stronger engine, rated at 380 bhp with a single Carter four-barrel and a mighty (and mighty convenient for the copywriters) 409 bhp with dual quads. Chevy sorted out production problems that had limited '61 supplies, and 15,019 big Chevys were equipped with the 409 for 1962. Thanks to the song—and thanks to its track performance—the big-block Chevy was a much-loved machine on Main Street, U.S.A.

The 1962 Chevrolet was certainly a good-looking home for any engine.

Bel Air

Discreet front fender emblems are the only clue to the presence of Chevy's "real fine" 409 V-8 in this '62 Bel Air Sport Coupe. The profile view reveals why this model's roofline has been nicknamed "slantback" in some circles. (Owner: Dan Mamsen)

Sheetmetal was only moderately changed from the previous year, but the results were particularly pleasing. A new Impala Sport Coupe with a convertible-like roofline was the year's popularity champ, but Chevy hedged its bets by leaving the 1961 "slant-back" roof on this year's Bel Air Sport Coupe. The year-old body style was retained in order to have a price-leading hardtop, but it was also aero-dynamically superior, just the thing for stock car racing. Chevrolet also made a point of reminding drag racers that the Bel Air was significantly lighter than a comparably equipped Impala. For those who were really serious about sanctioned racing, aluminum front-end components were available from the factory. Only 18 of the 409 Bel Airs were so equipped, and just one is known to survive today.

All across the nation the 409-powered Bel Airs hit the drag strips with a vengeance and were

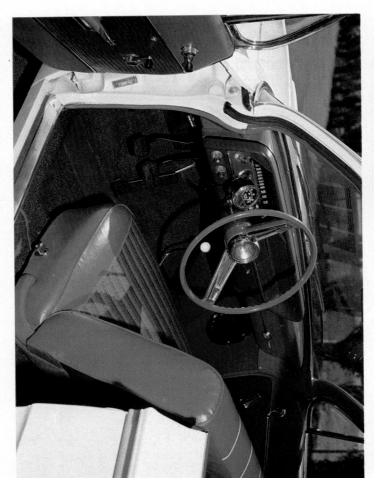

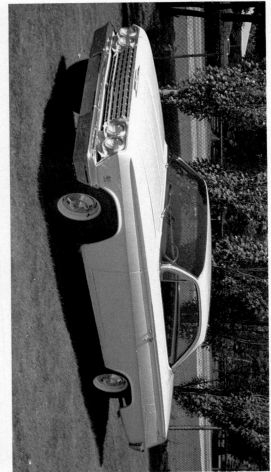

respected competitors wherever they went in '62. Dave Strickler and Hayden Proffitt were two well-known Bel Air pilots who, with a little help from Chevrolet, knew how to put a 409 in the winner's circle. Yet for all its success in the quarter-mile, the 409 was something of a stone on the banked ovals. A weak top end was too much for the Bel Air's "fast" roofline, especially when it had to run against the brutal 421 Pontiacs. But the 409 remained king of the street. That rumbling idle and the subtle "409" front fender flags signaled potent prestige wherever hot cars met.

One place where the Bel Air hardtop didn't shine was the showroom. While Impala Sport Coupe sales (including SS models) soared to 317,477 units, Bel Air Sport Coupe deliveries totaled just 5950. With the 409, the Bel Air was an exotic and rather expensive machine. Without it, most buyers saw no reason to prefer the Bel Air hardtop over the slightly more luxurious but considerably more expensive Impala version. Today it's an especially rare sight, and if you do spot one, chances are that it's not a 409. The standard 135-bhp "Hi-Thrift" six was far more popular, as were the 283 and new 327 small-block V-8s.

Even without 409 power, the '62 Bel Air remains a sharp, unusual Chevy with many practical virtues. There are spacious accommodations for six on comfortable bench seats, and the 'Deep-Well' trunk will handle more luggage than you're likely to ever need. In the more softly sprung, non-409 cars, those big coils really do serve up a "Jet-Smooth" ride. Thanks to the tremendous glass area, vision in all directions is terrific, although glare can be a problem through the wrap-over windshield. The vinyl/cloth interior was colorful, if not particularly durable. But no matter. Interior trim is readily available from aftermarket suppliers, and so are engine, chassis, and body parts. This is, after all, a Chevrolet.

Among the rarest of the rare, this '62 Bel Air 409 Sport Coupe has the racing-oriented, seldom-ordered factory aluminum front-end panels. It's likely the last surviving car with them. Appearance inside and out is deceptively plain. (Owner: Rusty Symmes)

CHEVROLET CORVETTE STING RAY 1963

When the first Polo White Corvette hit the streets in the summer of 1953, purists scoffed at its automatic transmission, "bathtub" styling, and "Blue-Flame" six-cylinder engine. But it didn't take long for Chevrolet to turn the Corvette into a real sports car. And when the first completely revamped generation arrived for 1963, even the 'Vette's detractors sat up and took notice.

Inspired by Bill Mitchell's Stingray racer of 1959-60, the 1963 Corvette Sting Ray was a styling showpiece and an engineering masterpiece. And for the first time, a Corvette coupe was available in addition to the familiar convertible roadster. Chassis design alone signaled a new era for Chevrolet's fiberglass-bodied sports car. Wheelbase was down four inches,

to 98, overall length was reduced slightly, and a new box-type frame contributed to a lower curb weight. The steel-reinforced cockpit was stronger and safer than before. Ride and handling qualities were substantially improved by the use of a new independent rear suspension with transverse leaf spring. A ball-joint front suspension and recirculating-ball steering with a mechanically adjustable ratio were retained from previous years. Front brake drums were wider, and all brakes were now self-adjusting. An alternator replaced the generator used previously.

While this Corvette boasted some pretty impressive specifications, it was the slinky bodywork that impressed enthusiast and non-enthusiast alike. Styling highlights included hidden

headlamps, peaked fenders and a generally tighter, racier appearance. From the outset, the fastback coupe with its stunning "boattail" roofline and split rear window design generated top interest. Zora Arkus-Duntov, the Corvette's outspoken, capable chief engineer, campaigned against the split window on the grounds that it would needlessly hamper visibility, but styling boss Mitchell considered it an essential part of the Sting Ray coupe character. The divider bar was gone for '64, thanks to Duntov's persistent lobbying—and howls from customers who com-

The sensational '63 Corvette Sting Ray in roadster form. (Chevrolet Motor Division)

plained they couldn't see out the window. Ironically, the divider bar, initially so unpopular, is the one feature that makes the '63 fastback worth more than any other Sting Ray on today's collector market.

The Sting Ray offered the same engine choices as the '62 Corvette, but the new chassis design and lower curb weight effectively created measurably improved performance. Chevy's respected 327-cid small-block V-8 re-

mained the basis of every Corvette performance option. *Boulevardiers* usually selected the standard 250-bhp engine, which could be teamed with standard 3-speed manual or extra-cost 4-speed manual or Powerglide

sales evenly divided between coupe and roadster. A new kind of buyer was now asking for creature comforts, and this new Corvette obliged with several options that bewildered dyed-in-the-wool sports car fanatics. Among these extra-cost niceties were leather upholstery, power steering, power brakes, AM/FM radio, tinted glass, and even air conditioning.

If buyers loved the Sting Ray—and they did—so did the contemporary motoring press. Writers raved about the improved driving position, the handling, and the looks. With its larger luggage compartment, the Corvette was finally a practical touring car. Unfortunately, the new model's high popularity created quality-control problems on the '63s.

Chevrolet updated and upgraded the Sting Ray in subsequent years. A hotter injected engine appeared for 1964, and the '65 got all-disc brakes and available big-block power. Styling was progressively cleaned up through 1967, the last year for this very special breed. But when Corvette enthusiasts are asked to choose their favorite Sting Ray, the 1963 split-window coupe is the one most often mentioned. Thanks to its dramatic, unique styling and bold engineering, this car will be remembered as one of the great Corvette designs of all time—and one of the great cars of the Sixties.

automatic transmission. For those who wanted more action—and most did—the 300-bhp 327 was popular at $53.80 extra. Corvette's most muscular carbureted engine was rated at 354 bhp, but the top option was the legendary 360-bhp 327 with ''Ramjet'' fuel injection, priced at a steep $430.40. With its ''fuelie'' test car, Car Life magazine achieved 0-60 mph in 5.9 seconds, the standing-start quarter-mile in 14.9 seconds, and 0-100 mph in 16.5 seconds. With the 3.70:1 rear axle ratio, top speed was an estimated 142 mph. Properly equipped, the new Corvette was a screamer.

Most Corvettes didn't go racing, but the machine was very capable at the track if you chose the right options. There was plenty of ''off-road'' equipment available, including heavy-duty suspension components, sintered-metallic brake linings, cast-aluminum

wheels with knock-off hubs, and a 36.5-gallon competition fuel tank.

The 1963 Sting Ray was an immediate hit. But it wasn't the race-car crowd that sent production to a record 21,613 units for the model year, with

Above: The 1963 Sting Ray marked the advent of the first closed Corvette, the curvy ''split-window'' coupe created by GM styling chief William L. Mitchell. Today, it's the most prized Sting Ray among collectors. (Chevrolet Motor Division). Left and right: The companion roadster was no less stunning. Rear-end styling was prefigured by the 1961-62 ''ducktail.'' (Owner: Mike Biederman)

CHEVROLET
CORVETTE 1968

In many ways the 1968 Corvette offered wild new styling, a trend-setting new body style, and improved handling. But it was also a Corvette steeped in controversy. Let's take a closer look at a design that was so good in so many ways that it remained in production largely unaltered for a full 15 years.

The fifth-generation Corvette was patterned after the experimental Chevrolet Mako Shark of 1965, much as the '63 Sting Ray had been inspired by a 1959 show/race car. Bill Mitchell supervised the design of all four, and he usually got what he wanted—except on the production '68.

The all-new styling was originally planned for 1967, but Corvette chief engineer Zora Arkus-Duntov was bothered by some aspects of the design and had it held back for a year, literally to smooth out the wrinkles. It seemed that the Mako-inspired front fenders were so high in the original prototype that they obscured the driver's forward view. So it was back to the styling studio for lower fender tops. The car that emerged looked sensational—low, sleek, and sexy—and it was because of this that the '68 would be the best-selling Corvette to date.

As before, there were two body styles, a coupe and a convertible. The coupe, however, was far different than the Sting Ray fastback that had preceded it, and it ushered in a new era in sporty car design. Chevrolet called it a "T-top." Its most intriguing feature was a pair of removable roof sections that offered the open-air feel of a convertible combined with the security of a full roll cage. The rear window was also detachable, thus affording true flow-through ventilation.

The convertible outsold the coupe for the last time in 1968, partly because production problems kept the closed model in limited supply until mid-model year. The convertible could be ordered with the standard soft top (in black, white, or beige) and with an extra-cost lift-off hardtop with glass rear window. A black-vinyl roof covering was available for the hardtop.

Under its new skin, the '68 Corvette was actually little changed from the 1963-67 Sting Ray. The same ladder-type frame, all-independent suspension, and drivetrains returned, though the wider body allowed use of 7-inch-wide wheels for the first time, which increased adhesion at high speeds. Tires were F70 x 15 wide-ovals supplied by various manufacturers.

Thanks to the new body's higher transmission tunnel, Corvette was finally able to take advantage of GM's excellent 3-speed Turbo Hydra-Matic. Previously, shiftless Corvettes were saddled with the rather inflexible twin-speed Powerglide. The automatic was now available with every engine offered save the highest-output 427s.

Engine choices were largely '67 carryovers, too. The standard unit was the familiar 327-cid V-8 with 300 bhp. For more small-block go, buyers had the option of choosing a 350-bhp version, but the emphasis this year was on the big-block engines, all 427's. With a four-barrel carburetor, the 390-bhp Turbo-Jet was a $200.15 option. When Chevrolet replaced that four-barrel with triple two-barrels, the price jumped to $305.50 and the bhp rating to 400. The most potent 427 listed was a 435-bhp monster that cost $437.10. Horsepower came cheap in 1968. There was another 427 rated at 435 bhp, Regular Production Option L-88. Priced at a whopping $947.90, it was a race mill pure and simple. To discourage its street use, Chevy refused to put a heater or a radio in any Corvette so equipped.

If the '68 Corvette's underpinnings weren't new, its interior most definitely was. Critics weren't happy. *Road & Track* magazine praised the driver/steering wheel relationship, but deployed the difficulty of getting in and out and complained about the location of the secondary gauges in the center of the dash, away from the driver's direct line of sight. Inadequate interior ventilation was also cited despite the incorporation of "Astro Ventilation" with dash-mounted vents. The tight-waisted appearance resulted in a narrower cockpit, the seating position was generally inferior to that of the 1963-67 design, and cabin appointments were too "space age" for

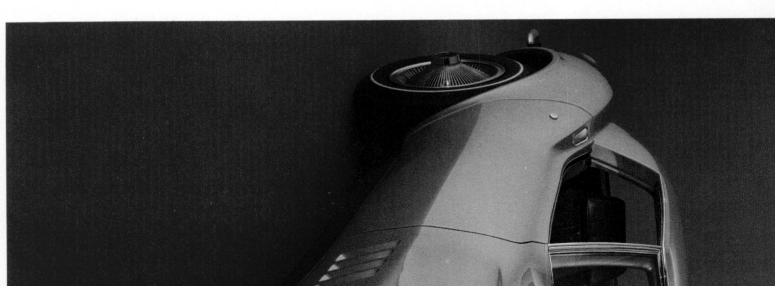

purists. Seats were all-vinyl buckets (genuine leather could be specified), and shoulder belts were standard on coupe models for the first time. As before, the small luggage area behind the seats was not accessible from outside. Also back there was a stowage area housing the battery, jack and tools, and a glove box (there was no dashboard locker).

Other complaints about the '68

centered on its harder ride and too many obvious lapses in workmanship. *Car and Driver* editor Steve Smith was particularly irked by his test '68: "Few of the body panels butted against each other in the alignment that was intended. Sometimes the pieces chafed against each other; sometimes they left wide gaps, sometimes they were just plain crooked." He also complained about a

The 1968 Corvette T-top coupe shows off its all-new Mako Shark-inspired styling in this well-known contemporary press photo. Chevy abandoned the Sting Ray name this year, then reinstated it as one word—Stingray—for 1969-76. The fifth generation would be the longest-lived Corvette design, lasting a full 15 years with two interim facelifts. Front grille was actually false. The real air intake was underneath, making this a "bottom breather." (Chevrolet Motor Division)

chronic water leak from the T-top and claimed that one of the door locks was so stiff that it bent the key. He termed all this "a shocking lack of quality control" and declared the car "unfit to road test." Proper cooling was also a problem with the big-block engines due to inadequate air flow through the small front under-bumper grille.

Critics may have had reservations about the '68 but the public loved it, and Corvette set a new sales record with 9936 coupes and 18,630 convertibles built for the model year. Adding to the new car's appeal was the fact that, at $4320 for the roadster, this Corvette was an uncommonly good value. Standard features included full instrumentation, hidden headlamps, four-wheel power disc brakes, backup lights, energy-absorbing steering column, wheel trim rings, and four-way

hazard warning flasher. For those who desired Cadillac-style luxury in a two-place sports car, the Corvette option list ran to power windows, power steering, air conditioning, AM/FM stereo, ski carrier, full wheel covers, whitewalls, and telescopic steering column. The more performance-minded were likely to forego some of these in favor of a close-ratio 4-speed transmission, 427 V-8, special suspension, heavy-duty brakes, off-road exhaust system, and Positraction. As always, this was a car for all tastes.

The 1968 Corvette was far from perfect. Besides the quality lapses, its relatively heavy construction was not something that endeared it to purists. But it was a commercial success, and its design—with improvements—would endure. It was arguably a better-handling machine than any Cor-

vette that came before and, with the proper equipment, it was unquestionably one of the fastest sports cars ever built. The T-top design was something that car companies everywhere have since copied.

For many years, the '68 has taken a back seat to the 1963–67 models in collector esteem. But that's changed because blinding acceleration, wild styling, and superb handling make the first of the "Sharks" a car to covet. And there's no longer any controversy about that.

Right: The '68 Corvette's sensuous lines are most evident in profile. Shown is the T-top coupe. (Chevrolet Motor Division) Below: Styling chief Mitchell poses with the '65 Mako Shark show car (left) and the production '68. (GM Design Staff)

CHEVROLET CAMARO 1968

In its first year, Chevy's Camaro established itself as the Ford Mustang's number-one competitor in the rapidly growing ponycar field. For 1968 it strengthened that position with increased sales volume. Camaro was a personal car that could be individualized through a myriad of option groups, packages, and accessories. No two would necessarily have to be alike, but

Chevy boasted each and every one of them as "The Hugger." Model year production reached 235,151, as Camaro was fast closing the gap on a pony that was tiring in the stretch.

As in debut 1967, Camaro was available as a hardtop coupe or convertible for '68. For those who wished to dress up the basic package a bit, the "Style Trim Group" added bright belt,

rocker, and wheel-lip moldings plus bright roof drip moldings on the coupe. The Rally Sport (or RS) package offered an even snazzier look for an additional $105.35. This option comprised Style Trim equipment plus a distinctive grille with hidden headlights, parking lights in the front valance panel, larger taillights, and black-painted rocker panel moldings.

Performance buffs were inclined to order the Super Sport (or SS) package with or without Rally Sport equipment. When you checked Camaro SS on the order form you got a 295-bhp, 350-cid small-block V-8, wide-profile red- or white-stripe tires, special suspension, a domed hood, "bumblebee" nose stripes, and SS identification. In mid-1968 the bumblebee stripes were replaced by a "sport stripe" that went around the nose and extended along the body-sides. To complement the new stripes, a special-edition Camaro was announced, available in four new colors:

LeMans Blue, Rallye Green, Brite Green, and Corvette Bronze. These cars were equipped with houndstooth upholstery, rear deck spoiler, whitewalls, and new mag-spoke wheel covers.

For the SS Camaro buyer who wanted more power than a potent small-block V-8 could deliver, Chevy offered three interesting big-block alternatives, all measuring 396 cubic inches. The first was rated at 325 bhp, the next at 350, and only a few lucky customers ordered and received a '68 Camaro with the 375-bhp L-78 V-8. Depending on engine selected, SS Camaros were equipped with 3-speed manual, 4-speed manual, Turbo Hydra-Matic or Powerglide transmissions.

Those who really had racing on their minds didn't go the SS route, however. There was another performance option for '68, promoted so quietly that many dealers didn't even know of its existence, one that turned a Camaro into a pony-killer: option number Z28. The Z28 package, offered only on the Sport Coupe, consisted of a specially modified 302-cid V-8 rated at a conservative 290 bhp, plus F41 sport suspension with 15 × 6-inch Corvette Rally wheels and wide-profile tires, along with special striping and quick steering. At $400.25, this had to

be one of the best performance buys of the decade. Front disc brakes were mandatory and four-wheel discs were optional. Production totaled only 7199. Many Z28s were raced successfully in the SCCA Trans-Am sedan series.

But most car buyers didn't go track racing, or even street racing, in 1968. They were more interested in style, reliability, and refinement. Camaro sold so well because it catered to the desires of these motorists, and did it with prices starting as low as $2638.

The base coupe, with Powerglide and the standard 250-cid six, was popular with the "supermarket set." Those who wished for a little more go-power usually opted for the 327-cid V-8, rated at 210 horsepower. Add a four-barrel carburetor and the rating jumped to 275. Of course, there were interior packages designed to complement the Rally Sport or Style Trim exterior groups, and by the time you ordered everything in the book, one window sticker was hardly enough.

Popular options included a $73 vinyl roof covering, $360 air conditioning, $31 Rally wheels, $100 power disc brakes, and Positraction at $42. But even with a generous helping of optional equipment, you really had to work to put a Rally Sport convertible over the $5000 mark.

In base trim, Chevy's 1968 Camaro convertible differed from the '67 only in a revised grille, resited backup lamps, side marker lights, and the absence of door vent wings. This car carries the optional "Style Trim Group" exterior dressup. (Owner: Robert Francek)

23

It takes a sharp eye to distinguish a 1968 Camaro from the similar '67, but Chevy buffs can do it in an instant...and so can you. Here are a few things to look for. Nineteen sixty-eight was the first year for side marker lights, vent windows disappeared in favor of flow-through "Astro

The '68 Camaro continued the '67's long-hood/short-deck proportions, typical of ponycars. Mini-spare tire saved space in the tiny trunk. This car's 210-bhp 327-cid V-8 provided good go in the relatively light Camaro, and was a popular option. (Owner: Robert Francek)

Ventilation," and non-RS cars had a new grille with rectangular parking lights. Inside were more dash padding, a new steering wheel, and a plusher optional Custom interior.

The value of a vintage Camaro is determined by several factors, including equipment, body style, and condition. A convertible is generally worth more than a hardtop, but not always. For example, an SS-equipped coupe will bring more money than a six-cylinder convertible with few options. A Z28 will bring top dollar among this year's Camaros, thanks to

its awesome capabilities and its reputation. Desirable options on any Camaro include the Rally Sport package, a 4-speed manual transmission, Custom interior, and any V-8.

Model year production was well over the 200,000 mark in 1968, but the vast number of available option packages makes *any* Camaro theoretically rare. Numbers aside, Chevy's first-generation ponycar is an exciting sportster that proved itself in competition and in the showroom. And that's why it's remembered today as one of the great cars of the Sixties.

CHRYSLER 300F 1960

Automotive historians remember 1960 mainly as the year of the Big Three compacts: Ford Falcon, Chevrolet Corvair, and Chrysler Corporation's Valiant. At the opposite end of the market, Chrysler offered up a memorable full-size flyer with a full measure of muscle, luxury, and style. It was the 300F, the sixth edition of a modern performance legend.

The 300F shared the all-new basic design of other '60 Chryslers, with unit construction, a revamped chassis, and clean new styling. Virgil Exner's beloved tailfins were still very much in evidence, but the F continued the elegant, chromeless theme that had made previous 300s such "Beautiful Brutes." In fact, Chrysler made a special attempt to explain the beauty of this car to its owners: "We believe the many admiring compliments you may already have received are proof

enough that an appreciation for unadorned, simple beauty of line is a growing trend in automotive taste. Your 300F achieves this by a classic grille opening and hood, a minimum of chrome trim on the side of the body, the use of single-tone painting, and the monochromatic natural leather interior with bucket seats." No mention was made of the simulated spare tire cover on the rear deck. Enthusiasts did complain loudly about that bit of styling overkill, and it disappeared on the 1961 successor model, the 300G. If the F was flamboyant even by 1960 standards, it was also much admired and very highly desired.

Like previous 300s, the F was a champion under the skin. This was a car designed by enthusiasts, and it showed. The suspension consisted of heavy-duty torsion bars and A-arms up front and a live rear axle on

specific-rate leaf springs. Standard quick-ratio power steering offered a level of precision unequalled by contemporary luxury cars. Complementing this "road" chassis was an engine that put the 300F in a class by itself. It was Chrysler's 413-cid V-8, then in its second year, with more mid-range punch thanks to a new ram-air induction system that provided a supercharging effect. With standard twin four-barrel carburetion, horsepower was rated at 375. If that wasn't enough, a 400-bhp version was also available.

At a time when most domestic cars were notoriously "under-tired," every

Chrysler styling was all-new for 1960, and the burly 300F was the cleanest expression of it. Distinctive "cross-hair" grille was unique to this model. (Owner: Vaughan Rose)

25

The F was the first 300 with four bucket seats, and the front ones swivelled out when the doors were opened to ease entry/exit. Standard 413-cid V-8 with ram induction was truly an impressive sight, and with up to 400 bhp it delivered equally impressive performance. Gimmicky decklid spare tire embossing detracted from the F's otherwise clean period styling. Note the special 300 wheel covers. (Owner: Vaughan Rose)

300F came with 9.00 × 15 Goodyear Blue Streak nylon tubeless whitewalls. Once again, a heavy-duty TorqueFlite with pushbutton controls was standard equipment, but a manual transmission was also available for the first time since 1956. Chrysler listed the French-built Pont-a-Mousson 4-speed unit as an option for the 300F, but only seven are known to have been installed and just one car so equipped is believed to have survived. The 4-speed cars were built primarily for racing, and they achieved noteworthy results. Andy Granatelli ran one up to 184 mph at Bonneville, and Gregg Ziegler put the 300F at the front of the stock class in the flying-mile competition at an average of 147 mph. *Motor Trend* magazine tried a stone-stock 300F with TorqueFlite and ran the quarter-mile in 16 seconds flat at a terminal speed of 85 mph. Tom McCahill of *Mechanix Illustrated* rated the 300F one of his all-time favorites.

The 300F was undoubtedly a powerhouse, but it treated its occupants lavishly. This was the first 300 with four individual buckets seats and full-length console with tachometer. The tach, mounted on the console and well out of the driver's line of sight, was rather superfluous with the Torque-Flite. Other gauges were located within the gaudy, futuristic "Astra-Dome" instrument panel. Color schemes were limited to preserve a tone of elegance. Beige leather was the only interior choice. Exterior hues were just Formal Black, Toreador Red, Alaskan White, and Terra Cotta. Two-tones were not available.

Even though 300 sales increased slightly for the model year, the F was truly a limited-production automobile. Only 1212 were built, 964 hardtops and 248 convertibles. The cars had tremendous enthusiast appeal but, at $5411 for the base hardtop, the market was somewhat limited. The ragtop started at $5841, which was more than most Cadillacs were going for in 1960.

The 300F was a unique, sophisticated car that didn't come cheap or cheaply, a car with substance that endures to this day. Later letter-series models were diluted by the advent of a non-letter series in the standard Chrysler line, as the marketing types sought to cash in on the great 300 nameplate. But in 1960 there was only one Chrysler 300, and it was the greatest performance car in the land.

DODGE POLARA 500 1962

The 1962 Polara 500 was four months late and 15 years early. Introduced at mid-model year, it was the most expensive series in a radically new Dodge line that was being clobbered by its more conventionally conceived competition. Had it appeared for 1977, Chrysler Corporation might not have come so close to extinction.

Although GM usually gets credit for the first downsized cars, Chrysler offered this "key to greater value" long before—and, unfortunately, long before the public was ready for it. Chrysler Corporation had high hopes for 1962. Its '61s had been poor sellers, and the '62s were supposed to spark showroom traffic, particularly

the all-new "standard" Plymouth and Dodge, which were now about the same size as Ford's new intermediate car, the Fairlane. The high hopes were quickly dashed as buyers stayed away in droves.

Dodge dealers were left confused, anxious, and without a genuine full-size car. Their slow-selling Valiant clone, the Lancer, was largely unchanged this year, and the big Polara and Matador were nowhere to be seen. In their place was a new Dart line priced dollar for dollar with Ford and Chevrolet. Problem was, these cars looked more like Valiants than Impalas, 10 inches shorter than the '61s and riding a 116-inch wheelbase, six

inches shorter than before. Dodge had gambled on sensible exterior dimensions and spacious accommodations for six inside. Benefits included better gas mileage and performance from smaller engines, plus improved handling. But the public literally wasn't buying this logic. Value was equated directly with size and weight, and the Dart looked about two sizes too small. To top it off, the Valiant-like styling was a bit too "unusual" for most tastes.

Dodge salvaged what it could from the '62 model year by instituting some quick fixes. Notable was the mid-year debut of the full-size Custom 880. Auto writers chuckled when they saw it: a 1962 Chrysler with a 1961 Polara

The bucket-seat Polara 500 topped the "standard" Dodge line for '62, and helped perk up lagging sales of these smaller full-size models. Besides this hardtop coupe, a convertible and hardtop sedan were also available. Dominating the colorful interior was a shiny but well laid out dash with full instrumentation (except for a tachometer) and Chrysler Corporation's then-customary pushbuttons for heater/defroster and automatic transmission. (Owner: Warren Emerson)

The full-sized Dodge was shrunk to intermediate proportions for '62 along with the standard Plymouths, and both model lines acquired somewhat odd styling inspired by Virgil Exner's design for the Plymouth Valiant/Dodge Lancer compacts. Thrusting trapezoidal grille and "A-frame" headlamp/tail-light positioning helped set the Dodge apart. Top-line Polara 500 carried a black air intake and contrasting full-length bodyside moldings, as well as a standard 361-cid V-8. (Owner: Warren Emerson)

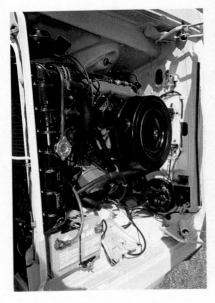

front end, arriving only months after the demise of the DeSoto. It may not have been original, but it did bring in some badly needed business. Of more interest to enthusiasts was a bucket-seat bomb placed at the top end of the floundering Dart line. The new car carried the familiar Polara badge, with a "500" attached for good measure, and it was available as a hardtop sedan, hardtop coupe, and convertible. While other Darts were usually equipped with a slant six or 318 V-8, the Polara packed a brawny 361-cid powerplant. Optional was a tire-burning 413-cid V-8 in 410- and 420-bhp versions. Besides all-vinyl buckets, every Polara 500 had dual exhausts, a padded instrument panel, and distinctive exterior trim, and front seat belt anchorage points.

With prices starting at $2960 for the hardtop sedan and $3019 for the coupe, the Polara 500 was not a bargain, but it sold: 12,268 units for the remainder of the model year. Younger buyers flocked to this new sporty Dodge, especially the convertible and two-door hardtop that not only looked fast but were. Drag racers appreciated the 413 V-8 in the lighter '62 body, and some were able to do some wonderful things with the combination.

The Polara 500 wasn't the only late-season entry intended to capitalize on the bucket-seat craze. Others included sister ship Sport Fury from Plymouth, Mercury's S/55, the Ford Galaxie 500/XL, and Buick's Wildcat. Every one offered more than 400 cubic inches. Bucket seats, big V-8s and fancy trim weren't enough to stop Dodge's sales from sliding, but the Polara 500 did add enough orders to keep Dodge in 9th place for '62. Plymouth did little better, ending the year in 8th place.

Dodge's real sales recovery didn't begin until 1963, when the Polara's wheelbase was stretched to a "standard" 119 inches. By 1965 a yacht-sized, gas-guzzling Polara was sitting pretty on a 121-inch wheelbase, where John Q. thought it should have been all along.

"Downsizing" wasn't part of our automotive vocabulary in 1962, so the virtues of that year's Dodge went unrecognized. Today, the '62 Polara seems far more rational than many of its "full-size" contemporaries, and it stands out as one of the great cars of the Sixties. Too bad it took us so long to realize it.

DODGE CORONET SUPER BEE 1968

Pontiac may have "invented" the muscle car in 1964, but it was Chrysler Corporation that put factory hot rods within the reach of those who could only dream about them before. When Plymouth bowed the first budget muscle car, the 1968 Road Runner, Dodge dealers cried "foul!" So in February, the "Good Guys" got one of their own, the Coronet Super Bee. Together, the two affordable street racers gave power back to the people. Dodge had a terrific car line for '68, and the public recognized this by buying a record 627,533 Darts, Coronets, Chargers, Polaras, and Monacos. Much of the action throughout the in-

dustry this year was in the mid-size arena, and the new Coronets and Chargers were powerfully persuasive reasons to choose Dodge. The Charger was reformed from an awkward fastback coupe into a slippery "flying buttress" notchback shaped like a NASCAR stocker, and sales soared. The family-oriented Coronet lost its breadbox styling, and the two-door versions were decidedly attractive.

Dodge had style for '68, but it had the "go" too, important in the mid-size market. This year's performance-oriented Dodges were the cars with the "bumblebee" stripes, each a member of the "Scat Pack." At first,

this group consisted of the compact 340-cid Dart GTS, the Coronet R/T hardtop and convertible, and the Charger R/T coupe. But with Plymouth scoring so well with the econo-priced Road Runner, Dodge demanded a duplicate for its dealers, and the mid-year Coronet Super Bee was the result.

Like the Road Runner, the Super Bee was a no-frills performance

"Double-delta" front-end treatment marked all '68 Dodge Coronets, but the low-price, high-performance Super Bee wore a special domed hood. (Owner: Mark Hanson)

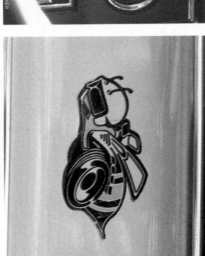

machine designed to be at home on the street or on the strip. It was essentially a base-level Coronet pillared coupe, with a strippo bench-seat interior and small hubcaps, decorated with Super Bee badges and those "bumblebee" stripes wrapped around

the rear deck. The excitement came in the form of a special four-barrel 383-cid V-8 that put out an honest 335 bhp at 5200 rpm. This high-winding powerplant was fortified with 440 Magnum V-8 heads and valvegear, a hot cam, and reworked manifolds.

Other Super Bee standards included dual exhausts, four-on-the-floor transmission with heavy-duty clutch, heavy-duty suspension and shocks, heavy-duty fade-resistant drum brakes, the Charger's "Rallye" instrumentation, and F70 × 14 wide-oval tires.

Dodge's Coronet Super Bee was an easy car to spot in 1968, thanks to its bright exterior colors, bold "bumblebee" tail stripes, and smooth, curvy lines. Standard equipment included the fully instrumented dashboard from this year's slick Charger hardtop, but the main attraction was a muscular 335-bhp 383-cid V-8. A considerably firmer chassis than found on workaday Coronets could be augmented with stylish Magnum 500 chrome wheels shod with fat wide-oval tires, as on this lovingly preserved beauty, which also sports the optional vinyl roof covering. Awesome hemi V-8 was available for prodigious performance, but relatively few Super Bees were so equipped. (Owner: Mark Hanson)

Despite all this, Super Bee prices started at under $3100. Dodge did it by replacing roll-down rear windows with the swing-out type, leaving off superfluous trim, and nixing things like consoles, bucket seats, and woodgrain appliques. The option list

did contain a few interesting items: a heavy-duty TorqueFlite automatic, power front disc brakes, road wheels, and Sure-Grip limited-slip differential. And then there was *the* legendary muscle car motor, the 426-cid Hemi. It was priced at a steep $831, so only few

Super Bees were equipped with it. Without slicks, a Super Bee 383 was almost as fast anyway, because the Hemi had too much sheer power for normal street tires to handle. Even with the 383, a Super Bee could cut a 0–60 mph time of under seven seconds.

The awesome 440 Magnum V-8 with triple two-barrel carburetion was offered in a special model called the Six-Pack, and Super Bee went on to have its best year on record.

A number of forces conspired to drive Super Bee sales down in model year 1970. The most crucial were skyrocketing insurance rates for all muscle cars in general, and a renewed interest in smaller, more ''sensible'' performers such as the fast-selling Duster 340. Perhaps worst of all, the '70 Super Bee was saddled with a peculiar facelift marked by an awkward double-loop front bumper/grille and an uninspired rear deck treatment.

For '71, the Super Bee was demoted to a performance package for the base Charger coupe. The next year it was gone, and that was too bad.

The Super Bee never really disappeared, though, dominating the nation's dragstrips well into the Seventies. Remaining examples are too valuable to be flogged like that anymore, so they've been retired as champions. Collectors treasure them all, but it's that original '68 coupe that's most in demand today, for it is the essence of the Super Bee concept. You know what that is: fun!

The Super Bee was a highly successful new entry for Dodge, and it contributed to the division's position as a leader in 1968's all-important youth market. Offerings were expanded for 1969 to include a hardtop coupe, and several new luxury options appeared.

''Double-delta'' theme was repeated in the '68 Coronet back panel, set off on the Super Bee by black accents. Standard 335-bhp V-8 looked unassuming under the hood, but endowed the relatively light Super Bee with satisfying performance. Initial base list price was a very affordable $3027. (Owner: Mark Hanson)

DODGE CHARGER DAYTONA 1969

Slippery shapes help cars of the Eighties go farther on a gallon of gas. Fuel efficiency wasn't a big concern in the energy-rich Sixties, but aerodynamics did play a role in automotive design back then. Witness the wild creature on these pages, a 1969 Dodge Charger Daytona. Although it can't fly, it looks like it should. The Daytona was designed solely for winning races on the NASCAR Grand National circuit, so 505 production examples were built to classify it as a "stock car" under the rules. Each started out as a normal R/T hardtop. Creative Industries of Detroit did the rest.

MoPar buffs lucky enough to find a Daytona at their local Dodge dealer must have been startled by the "Batmobile" styling. The slippery snout and huge rear wing were its main features, designed to boost top speed up to the 190-mph bracket on the track. They were only of psychological importance on the street. Other Daytona equipment included the 440-cid Magnum V-8 with four-barrel carb and dual exhausts, TorqueFlite automatic, all-vinyl bucket seats, F70 × 14-inch red-line tires, the R/T handling package, rear bumper guards, concealed headlights, flush backlight, carpeting, "bumblebee" stripes, and quick-fill gas cap. The list price for this exotica was about $4000.

With its anteater snout, the Daytona measured a whopping 226.5 inches end to end, two inches longer than a '69 Chrysler New Yorker! Obviously, this car was more at home on the open road than it was fighting for a parking spot in downtown traffic. Wheelbase was 117 inches and width 76.6. For those who considered the 440 Magnum too puny, the legendary 426 hemi-head V-8 was an available option. Bobby Isaac tested a Hemi Daytona for Dodge and offered a few

Winged Warrior: The 1969 Dodge Charger Daytona. (Chrysler Historical Collection)

interesting observations: "Well, there's one obvious thing about a Charger Daytona. Nobody, but nobody, walks by without breaking his neck to take a second look. Old Slippery has a snout that strikes out a country mile in front, and an adjustable spoiler that looks two stories tall in the rear." Issac went on to confirm the well-known belief that the Hemi wasn't a pussycat: "Now the Hemi may idle like a coffee can full of rocks, and it may need a wrench applied a little more often than usual. On the other hand, as far as acceleration is concerned, the Hemi turns on where the others shut off." The Hemi was rated at 425 bhp, but its actual output was closer to 475—and that was in *street* tune.

While the production Daytona looked like a full-blown racer outside, its interior was several shades plusher than you'd see in a Grand National car. The bucket seats were straight out of the Charger R/T, and appointments ran to wall-to-wall carpeting, full instrumentation within a padded dash, electric clock, and a three-spoke steering wheel with partial horn ring. Op-

tions included an engine dress-up kit, a high-rise manifold and carb, and performance gear ratios. Dodge dealers were very accommodating in the Sixties.

NASCAR Daytonas did without fancy interiors, of course, and they managed to rewrite the record book. Despite a serious challenge from wind tunnel-shaped Ford Talledegas and Mercury Cyclone Spoilers, the Daytona was recognized as the fastest stock car in the world. Dodge race fans must have been pleased to see a Daytona win at Daytona International Speedway in February 1969, where it was the first stocker to average a 200-mph lap. The incredible Daytona won 80 percent of the races it entered in its short career, and helped Dodge take 22 Grand National victories during the '69 season.

Dodge dropped the Daytona after 1969, but Plymouth picked up the pieces and created the 1970 Road Runner Superbird. The Superbird used an extended snout and deck spoiler that were similar to but not interchangeable with the parts used on the Daytona.

Plymouth built about 2000 Superbirds, making them less desirable to collectors than the rarer Daytonas.

NASCAR outlawed both winged warriors in 1971, but it didn't matter much by that time anyway. A new Charger with closer kinship to the garden-variety Coronet replaced the brutal 1968-70 generation, and jacked-up insurance rates were steering customers away from muscle cars.

Today's MoPar enthusiasts remember the rare 1969 Dodge Daytona with a special reverence. It packed a wallop, and flaunted it. Never again will there be a "production" car like the Daytona, and never again will a Grand National stock car be so closely related to an everyday automobile.

Right: Driver Bobby Isaac poses with the Charger Daytona he campaigned in 1969. The car's towering wing and extended snout are quite evident in this view. Above: Isaac's racing Charger Daytona and the production version. Only 505 of the latter were built. (Chrysler Historical Collection)

FORD THUNDERBIRD
SPORTS ROADSTER 1963

Ford built its last two-seat Thunderbird in 1957. The car's thousands of enthusiasts mourned its passing and cringed when they saw its four-place successor. But many thousands of others viewed the '58 in an entirely different light. To them it was a sexy new 'Bird with a back seat, and sales reached heights that Ford had only dreamed of with the two-seater. So much for the enthusiasts.

But a funny thing happened on the way to the Sixties. Early 'Bird values actually started climbing at a time when other five-year old cars were about as desirable as yesterday's newspaper. Ford Division general manager Lee Iacocca took note of the situation, briefly studied the feasibility of returning the 1957 model to production, and finally decided to offer a two-seat sport derivative of the third-generation 1961-63 design.

The idea was good and the execution terrific. Working on a decidedly low budget and with instructions not to make any sheetmetal revisions, the design team came up with a nifty solution. Arriving for model year 1962, it was not a two-seat sports car in the strictest sense—certainly nothing like the 1955-57 Thunderbird—but the two-seat *effect* was readily apparent. It was created simply by installing a cleverly crafted fiberglass tonneau cover over the convertible's rear seat area. Omitting the standard rear fender skirts and adding a set of stunning Kelsey-Hayes wire wheels completed the package. Manufactured by one of Ford's Canadian suppliers, the tonneau could be easily removed for four-passenger seating. With it in place, the Thunderbird convertible was absolutely transformed. With appearance that was genuinely exciting, this was the first 'Bird since the '57 to attract the enthusiast's eye. Ford called it the Sports Roadster. Besides the sleek tonneau (which incorporated front seat headrests) and the wire wheels, the new model featured distinctive front fender insignia, a passenger grab bar, and brushed-aluminum interior trim.

The rear fender skirts were left off because they wouldn't fit over the wire wheels. Power was provided by a 390-cid "Thunderbird" V-8 rated at 300 bhp. A triple two-barrel version rated at 340 bhp cost $242.10. Only 120 of the 1962 Sports Roadsters were fitted with this option. Cruise-O-Matic was the standard and only available transmission.

The Sports Roadster was unquestionably an exciting addition to the Thunderbird line, and it was prominently displayed in Ford advertising. Yet sales reached just 1427 units. The problem was price. While the standard convertible listed for $4788, the roadster was a steep $5439 without options, a lot of money for a fake two-seater.

Below: The Thunderbird Sports Roadster in its initial 1962 form. Normal rear fender skirts were left off to clear the standard Kelsey-Hayes wire wheels. (Ford Motor Co.). Right: The '63 Sports Roadster flips its lid, a maneuver possible with the special tonneau cover in place. Note revised door trim. (Owner: John Hruby)

Ford didn't give up on the Sports Roadster, however, and returned it for '63 prettier than ever. Styling changes were subtle, but most observers agreed that they gave the car added flair. The most noticeable change was the addition of prominent bodyside creaselines that wrapped around new door ornamentation. The price was up, to $5563, but the long list of standard equipment included Thunderbird's famous Swing-Away steering wheel, power steering, power brakes, all-vinyl bucket seats, center console, and electric clock. New features for '63 were an alternator, optional AM/FM push-button radio, and extended maintenance intervals. Popular options included leather upholstery ($106.20), air conditioning ($415.10), narrow-band whitewall tires ($42.60), and power windows ($106.20). Although ordinary Thunderbirds could be ordered in 20 exterior hues, the Sports Roadster was available only in Raven Black, Silver Mink, Champagne, Rangoon Red, Corinthian White, Diamond Blue, Sandshell Beige, and Chestnut. Convertible tops were black, white, or blue, depending on body color. The optional 340-bhp V-8 was initially offered, but was withdrawn in early 1963, and only 37 of this year's Sports Roadsters were so equipped.

Sports Roadster production declined drastically in '63 to just 455 copies. The model was dropped from the restyled '64 lineup, although a similar tonneau cover was offered as a dealer accessory. Again, few were sold.

Time has treated the Sports Roadster better than the public did. In its day, it wasn't accepted as a true successor to the beloved 1955-57 'Birds, but today it rivals the earlier cars in value and is arguably the prettiest of the post-1957 models. Lower production has made the 1963 version more desirable — and expensive — than the '62 on the collector market, but either one will rank near the top of the average 'Bird-lover's most-wanted list. With its sports car flair and rarity unequalled among Thunderbird convertibles, the Sports Roadster still lives up to a former T-Bird advertising slogan: "Unique in all the World."

Sports Roadster frontal styling and cockpit were similar to those of other 1961-63 Thunderbirds. Engine compartment on this '63 has been considerably brightened up. (Owner: John Hruby)

FORD GALAXIE 500/XL 1964

The full-size Ford Galaxie 500/XL was the cornerstone of a product line that won *Motor Trend* magazine's Car of the Year award in 1964. Though they weren't all-new and represented no significant engineering or aesthetic breakthroughs, they went home with the gold. The reason was performance, and Ford's emphasis on it was total.

The big Ford's performance renaissance really began in early 1962 with introduction of the high-output 406-cid V-8 and the bucket-seat Galaxie 500/XL series. Stock car racers approved of the new V-8, but the XL's Thunderbird-style roofline caused aerodynamic

problems that limited top speed on NASCAR supertracks. Salvation arrived for "1963½" in the form of a semi-fastback Sports Hardtop body style. For good measure, a muscular new 427-cid V-8 appeared at the same time. As Ford started winning races, XL sales started taking off.

Refinement was the key word for 1964. Though this chassis design was now five years old, it worked best this year. The effective semi-fastback rooflines returned, and lower body panels on all big Fords got a fresh look. Interiors were updated with thin-shell all-vinyl bucket seats, new trim patterns, and several new color combina-

tions. The readable instrument panel was largely unchanged from 1963. Front seat belts were standard on all cars built after January 1, 1964.

The 1964 XL could be ordered three ways: hardtop coupe, convertible, and hardtop sedan. The hardtop coupe was the favorite, with 58,306 deliveries. Next came the convertible at 15,169 sales. Only 14,661 buyers chose the four-door. Standard equipment included an all-vinyl interior that would

Hardtop coupe was the most popular Galaxie 500/XL for '64. (Ford Motor Co.)

put a Super Sport Impala to shame, console-mounted transmission shifter, and spinner-type full wheel covers. Lesser Galaxies were available with an anemic 232-cid "Mileage Maker" six, but the XL's base engine was a 289-cid V-8 rated at 195 bhp. The next step up was a 352 V-8 with 250 bhp, but most

Above: Console and new "thin shell" front buckets were 500/XL standards. Below: The big Fords' fresh lower-body sheetmetal for '64 gave the Galaxie 500/XL convertible a new look. (Ford Motor Co.)

XLs left the factory with one of two 390-cid V-8s, rated at 300 and 330 bhp. All-out race car performance was the identifying feature of Ford's two top engine options, both measuring 427 cubic inches. With a single four-barrel carburetor, the horsepower rating was 410; with dual quads it was 425. The 427 Galaxies were equipped with heavy-duty suspensions, larger brakes, and 15-inch wheels. When full wheel covers were ordered on these cars they were modified 1956 Mercury discs. The big-block big Ford was as impractical

for street use as it was successful on the race track. Its real mission was to dominate Grand National competition, and Ford managed to put the '64 Galaxie in the winner's circle more often than any other car that year.

Race-prepared Galaxies may have been crowd pleasers, but the 1964 Fords pleased a lot of people in the showrooms, which is where it really counted. Production was second only to Chevrolet, and Ford's model year total rose substantially compared to 1963, a rousing 923,232 units.

XL base prices were reasonable ($3222 for the two-door hardtop), but most of these cars were heaped with extra-cost luxury and performance equipment. Popular options included 4-speed manual transmission (standard with the 427 V-8), AM radio, tinted glass, air conditioning, narrow-band whitewall tires, vinyl top, power steering, and power brakes. The Thunderbird-inspired Tilt-Away steering wheel was available, but rarely ordered.

The full-size Ford was completely redesigned for 1965, but collectors don't see it as an improvement over the venerable '64. Maybe it's because the luxury-laden LTD series replaced the XL as Ford's top dog, or maybe it's because the conservative styling was devoid of the flair that marked the 1963–64 Galaxies. How ironic then that 1965 was Ford's greatest year ever in NASCAR, with 48 wins out of the scheduled 55 events.

FORD MUSTANG 2+2 1965

The 1965 Ford Mustang was a revolution on wheels. Here was a uniquely styled personal car for those who thought (or were) young, with prices that started at just $2368. Mustang quickly became the third best-selling single car line in the land and the automotive phenomenon of the Sixties.

Purists insist otherwise, but technically there was no "1964½" Mustang. The car was announced on April 17, 1964, for the 1965 model year. Mustang's arrival was heralded with cover stories in both *Time* and *Newsweek*, and the sprightly new pony was selected pace car for the 1964 Indianapolis 500. Everybody loved the Mustang. Initial body styles were limited to a notchback coupe and convertible, with an equally limited selection of high-performance features. The base engine was an anemic 170-cid six

straight out of the Falcon, and a 260-cid 164-bhp V-8 or 289-cid 210-bhp V-8 were the only options. But more variety—and more muscle—was on the way.

When the rest of the Ford line changed over to 1965 production in August '64, Mustang received some notable revisions. A 200-cid six replaced the 170 as standard equipment and the 260 was dropped in favor of a 200-bhp 289. The top two 289-cid options were rated at 225 and 271 bhp, and an alternator replaced the previous generator. Newly available functional features included front disc brakes and a set of especially attractive styled steel wheels. But the biggest news was the introduction of a new model, the fastback 2+2.

The 2+2 added something of a European flavor to the line, and more

than one early '65 notchback was traded for the sexy new coupe. Other Mustangs made do with a shallow, short trunk, but the fastback offered a novel twist *a la* Plymouth's Barracuda. The rear seat folded down and a divider panel swung out of the way, providing uninterrupted floor space from the rear bumper to the back of the front seats.

The base 2+2 was priced at $2589. That included the 200-cid six, Silent-Flo ventilation, and a tinted rear window. Popular extras included 4-speed manual transmission, AM radio, whitewall tires, and Rally Pac, a $70.80 clock and tachometer.

In April 1965 a new option group

This particular 1965 Mustang 2 + 2 is a base six-cylinder model and a former restoration project car for the editors. Early Mustang styling still looks good 20 years later.

43

was announced that added even more sizzle to red-hot Mustang sales. Called the GT Equipment Group, it was available for any Mustang at a $165.03 surcharge. The GT package, available with either of the four-barrel 289 V-8s, comprised dual exhausts exiting through the rear valance panel, a special handling package, front disc brakes, grille-mounted fog lamps, five-gauge instrument cluster, and GT side stripes.

An Interior Decor Group ($107.08) and full-width bench seat with folding center armrest ($24.43) were also made available in mid-1965. The bench seat wasn't popular, but the fancy interior package was preferred by customers who wanted a Thunderbird at a fraction of the cost.

A dream Mustang, then or now, would be a '65 fastback with the GT Equipment Group, styled steel wheels, "pony" interior, a full load of other optional equipment, and the available "K" engine. The "K" was the 271-bhp 289, installed in only 6996 of the '65 models. With actual horsepower considerably higher than advertised, this factory hot-rodded 289 didn't come cheap, an astronomical $435.80. That's why so many more GTs were equipped with the 225-bhp 289 at $162 extra.

For some, even the "GT-K" wasn't enough Mustang. Enter Carroll Shelby. 'Ol Shel took 500 of the new '65 fastbacks, outfitted them for competition, and sold them to enthusiasts who wanted something a little different and a lot more potent. Called GT-350, it was stripped of all non-functional ornamentation, rear seat, and steel hood. A fiberglass hood with functional scoop was substituted, and a wood-rim racing steering wheel, special suspension, competition disc brakes, Koni racing shocks, and Goodyear 7.75 × 15 Blue Dot racing tires were added. Horsepower jumped to 306 with installation of a high-flow Holley four-barrel carburetor, high-rise aluminum manifold, tubular headers, and a straight-through glass-pack exhaust system. The GT-350 cost over $4500 and was hardly suited for everyday use, but it's now the most valuable Mustang of them all.

The standard '65 fastback was more streetable, affordable, and far more popular, with 77,079 deliveries for the model year. Today you can have one for less than $10,000—if you hurry.

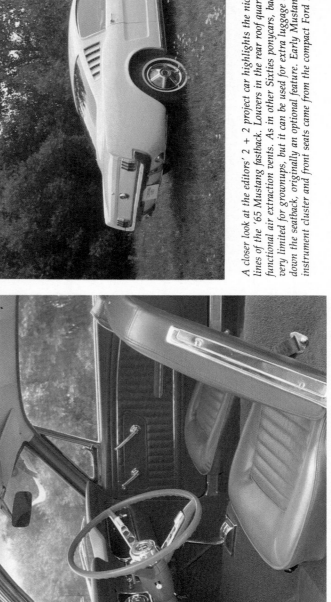

A closer look at the editors' 2 + 2 project car highlights the nicely balanced lines of the '65 Mustang fastback. Louvers in the rear roof quarters served as functional air extraction vents. As in other Sixties ponycars, back seat space is very limited for grownups, but it can be used for extra luggage by flipping down the seatback, originally an optional feature. Early Mustangs' standard instrument cluster and front seats came from the compact Ford Falcon.

FORD MUSTANG
BOSS 429 1969

The 1969 Boss 429 was the mightiest Mustang of all. Pony performance had come a long way since the spring of 1964, when Mustangs rolled off the line with small sixes and small-block V-8s, but who would have ever thought it would come to this?

In the late Sixties it wasn't clear whether Ford ruled performance or whether Ford ruled performance or performance ruled Ford. A high-

output 289 V-8 was the Mustang's largest and most powerful engine for 1966. The next year, Mustang put on weight and inches in order to make room for a boat-anchor 390 V-8. A 427-cid V-8 was offered on a limited basis for '68, and a 428 Cobra-Jet unit was announced mid-year.

A brand-new Mustang arrived for 1969, and once more it was a bigger car. The model range included the

traditional convertible and two-door hardtop plus a stunning new 2+2 with full fastback styling, named Sports-Roof. Luxury lovers were enticed by the plush new Grandé hardtop. The star of the show was the Mach 1 SportsRoof, available with a choice of five engines ranging from a two-barrel 351 to the Cobra-Jet 428. It was suitably striped and scooped for the correct performance image. But that

wasn't enough for Bunkie Knudsen, fresh from GM and newly installed as Ford president. The former Pontiac chief was a great believer in muscle machines and had no real affection for the early, mild-mannered Mustang.

Debuting in mid-1969 was the Boss 302, several shades hotter than the Mach 1 and designed to compete against the Camaro Z28 on the SCCA's Trans-Am circuit. It was also designed to win, and it would. Equipment included a 302-cid V-8 rated at 290 horsepower (actual output was closer to 350), 4-speed manual transmission, 3.50:1 rear axle ratio, special suspension, quick steering ratio, flared front fenders, and special striping. Only 1934 were built. But though the Boss 302 was the hottest production Mustang to date, it still

wasn't hot enough. The Boss 429 was.

The legendary Boss 429 Mustang was born through a curious set of circumstances. In order for Ford to qualify its 429 hemi-head V-8 for NASCAR competition, it had to be installed in 500 production cars. Although the NASCAR racers were Torinos, Ford decided to side-step the rules committee by offering a street version of the big-block in the smaller Mustang. The decision must have been made in a moment of madness—glorious madness.

The 429 V-8 was too large to fit even the larger '69 Mustang, so a special assembly line was set up to shoehorn these engines into selected Sports-Roofs. Required modifications were made to front suspension and fenders, and standard track was widened.

Other Boss 429 features included a functional hood scoop, a specific front spoiler, F60 × 15 tires, Magnum 500 chrome wheels, heavy-duty suspension, engine oil cooler, power steering, and power disc brakes. A Traction-Lok differential with 3.91 gearing helped get all that torque to the pavement. The battery was put in the trunk, mainly because it took up so much space up front. This no-nonsense machine was decked out with graphics far more subtle than the Mach 1 and Boss 302 striping packages. Boss 429 decals on the front fenders were the

Though bereft of loud striping, the '69 Mustang Boss 429 did carry an aggressive hood scoop, necessary to clear its big-block V-8. (Owner: Greg Turley)

only giveaway.

The interior seemed another con-tradition. A Decor Group, optional on other models, was included on every Boss 429, along with high-back bucket seats, deluxe seat belts, center console, and woodgrain instrument panel. A "Visibility Group" included parking brake warning lamp, glove box lock, and luggage compartment, ash tray, and glove box lights.

Automatic transmission and air condi-tioning were not available, and color choices were restricted to Raven Black, Royal Maroon, Candy Apple Red, Wimbleton White, Blue, and Black Jade.

The Boss cost $4798, making it the most expensive non-Shelby Mustang to date. Only 858 were built for model year 1969. Another 498 were built to '70 specifications. Mustang became larger and heavier for '71 and thus

Above: Massive 429 V-8 was a real shoehorn fit in the '69 Mustang engine room. The large chrome tubes are actually braces to help maintain structural rigidity in hard acceleration. (Owner: Greg Turley)

even further removed from the original '65. One reason it swelled was so that the 429 could be installed on the nor-mal assembly line. But performance cars were on the wane by this time and only a limited number of detuned 429s made it into Mustangs that year. The next year, the big-inch engine was gone from Ford's ponycar line.

A further irony is that the Boss 429 was actually slower in 0–60 mph and quarter-mile contests than the Boss 302 and even the 351 Mach 1. The engine was potent enough, but the chassis and tires just weren't up to the job. The Boss 429 made a fearsome starting point for those who wished to modify, but it was a disappointing performer out of the box.

The Boss 429 represented a concept gone wild, and was partly responsible for production Mustangs that got big-ger instead of better in the 1970s. But it was Ford's ultimate weapon in the Sixties performance wars—and one of the decade's most memorable machines of any kind.

Wide brushed-aluminum side trim continued to mark the Starfire in its encore 1962 guise. The two-door hardtop was a new companion offering for the original '61 convertible. (Owner: Jack Henning)

OLDSMOBILE STARFIRE 1962

Oldsmobile capitalized on the trend towards full-size sportsters in mid-1961 with the stunning Starfire. This chrome-encased, leather-trimmed convertible was an immediate success, so offerings were expanded for '62 to include a hardtop coupe. In response to dealer criticism that the 1961 looked too small, all big Oldsmobiles were lengthened for '62. Rear-end styling was simplified, but an elaborate, two-tier grille gave the front end a unique new look. The full-size line included the volume-leading Dynamic 88 series, the plusher and more powerful Super 88, the longer and more luxurious Ninety-Eight, and the Starfire. Olds prices started at $2403 for the compact F-85 coupe, but

the Starfire hardtop listed at an impressive $4131 and the companion convertible was the most expensive offering in the entire line, with a base of $4744.

If that was a lot of 1962 dollars, the Starfire was a lot of 1962 car. Standard equipment included color-keyed leather-trimmed front bucket seats, a center console housing the floor-mounted Hydra-Matic shift lever, plus power steering, power brakes, dual exhausts, carpeted luggage area, and color-keyed wheel covers. Every Starfire came with a console-mounted tachometer, and the convertibles left the Lansing factory with special mufflers, power windows, power seats, and whitewall tires. Rocket V-8 power

was nothing new at Olds in '62, but the Starfire boasted the largest standard engine in Olds history. Also called Starfire, the big 394-cid V-8 packed a powerful 345 bhp at 4600 rpm and demanded lots of premium gas thanks to a 10.5:1 compression ratio.

The Starfire was easily differentiated from lesser Oldsmobiles by a wide band of brushed-aluminum side trim and a distinctive grille. The interior was flashy even by '62 standards, with lots of chrome accents, a ribbon-type speedometer, aluminum-accented carpet inserts, and a custom-styled sport steering wheel.

But glitter and go weren't the Starfire's only endearing qualities. The 4200-pound car was 213 inches long

and every inch an Oldsmobile. The division's rugged "Guard-Beam" frame design assured protection in side impacts, and the finned brake drums had a fairly generous 197.7 square inches of lining area. Tire size was 8.00 × 14 on the hardtop

and 8.50 × 14 on the convert.

The basic Starfire was lavishly equipped, but few went out the door for less than $5000. Popular options included "Guide-Matic" automatic headlight dimmer, power trunklid release, air conditioning, power vent

GM's 1962 B-body two-door hardtops carried convertible-like "bows" in the upper rear roof area, and the Starfire was no exception. Inside, Oldsmobile's bucket-seat biggie boasted lots of bright trim and ample room for four or five adults. Center console housed shift lever and a tachometer. Note protective chrome strips on the floor and the color-keyed all-vinyl upholstery of this beauty. (Owner: Jack Henning)

windows, power antenna, radio, and seat belts. Quality features Olds boasted about for '62 included factory-sealed chassis lubrication, self-adjusting brakes, and an improved Hydra-Matic. But critics still complained about the automatic transmission's abrupt shift quality and its unorthodox "PNDSLR" shift quadrant. Olds may have been obliquely referring to rough shifting action when it called Hydra-Matic "the performance transmission with the solid feel." There can be no doubt that the Starfire V-8/Hydra-Matic combination did offer "rocketing get-up and go...combined with an exceptionally authoritative passing gear!"

The carryover Starfire convertible generated 7149 retail orders, down slightly from the 7800 sales recorded in 1961. The new hardtop more than took up the slack, however, with 34,839 finding homes. The new "like-a-convertible" roofline, shared with other GM full-size two-door hardtops,

may have been responsible for the brisk sales rate, or it may have been the handsome good looks that were Starfire's alone. But the big bucket-seat Olds would never do so well again. Sales plunged for 1963 and declined every year until the model's demise after 1966. Part of the reason was competition in the arena where Olds had been a pioneer. The clean-lined 1963 Pontiac Grand Prix claimed record sales partly at the Starfire's expense, and Buick's Wildcat and Riviera also took a toll. By 1966 the Starfire was all but forgotten in the hoopla surrounding that year's new front-drive Toronado, which essentially replaced it. But the Starfire was the sportiest and

most elegant way to go Oldsmobile in 1962. In the sales folder handed out at dealerships, prospects read about "the personal sense of pride as you quietly tell a parking lot attendant, 'Mine's the '62 Olds.'" Today, more than two decades later, lucky Starfire owners still know that feeling.

OLDSMOBILE

JETFIRE 1963

In the fuel-conscious Eighties, turbocharging has proven to be a reliable way of getting V-8-like performance from a small-displacement four-cylinder engine. Many manufacturers have shown interest in the idea over the years, and Chrysler Corporation alone built more than 100,000 turbo-equipped cars just for model year 1984. Only Chevrolet and Oldsmobile seem reluctant to embrace the concept. And that's ironic, because in mid-1962 both made industry news by bringing out turbocharged "sports cars." Chevy's entry was the well-known Corvair Monza Spyder with a rear-mounted flat-six. Oldsmobile's contender was several degrees hotter than the Spyder but never enjoyed its notoriety. Interestingly, it's relative obscurity that has endeared this car to discriminating collectors of special-interest Oldsmobiles. Of course, we're talking about the F-85 Cutlass Jetfire.

The Jetfire arrived as a high-performance option package available only for the two-door Cutlass hardtop coupe. Its heart was a turbocharged version of the 215-cid aluminum V-8 that Olds had been using in the F-85/Cutlass since model year 1961, when its first compact debuted. The Jetfire's turbocharger provided a power boost of almost 40 percent. A high 10.25:1 compression ratio was made possible by using a unique water-injection system, which squirted fluid into the gas mixture to control internal cylinder temperatures. The result was 215 bhp, the magic one horsepower per cubic inch. But Jetfire production stopped at a disappointing 3765 units for 1962. Olds planned a big push for '63 to further test public reaction to its turbocharged compact.

The 1963 Cutlass/F-85 line was restyled for a bigger, more important look. The new models looked a lot like a scaled-down Dynamic 88, especially from the rear, and that was intentional. The market was swinging back to big cars in the early Sixties, and the

last thing Olds wanted was a compact that looked too compact.

At $3048, the Jetfire was the priciest of the small Oldsmobiles, and this year it acquired new styling distinction to stand apart from everyday Cutlass hardtops. Outside it wore flamboyant Starfire-like bodyside and rear deck trim. Inside were all-vinyl bucket seats, borrowed from the Cutlass, and bold Jetfire identification on dashboard and door panels. Other interior touches included a center console containing the shift lever for the standard 3-speed manual transmission as well as a boost gauge for the "Turbo-Rocket" V-8. A fully synchronized 4-speed manual and Hydra-Matic transmissions were optional. Standard equipment included full wheel covers, dual exhausts, an aluminized muffler, and a 3.36:1 rear axle ratio. Tire size was 6.50 × 13.

The Jetfire's compact dimensions and unusual powerplant made it especially interesting to car buffs and rallyists. Wheelbase was just 112 inches, overall length was 192.2 inches, and weight was a svelte 2618 pounds. With the aforementioned 215 bhp on tap, it was remarkably quick. Enthusiast magazines timed the Jetfire at around 8.5 seconds from rest to 60 mph and recorded top speeds of over 105 mph. There was only one other 1963 compact that even came close and that was the 326 V-8 Pontiac Tempest, which shared the Jetfire's underbody structure. Pontiac engineers knew that the heavy 326 V-8 was too much engine for the lightweight compact, but buyers snatched up the nose-heavy Tempests and all but ignored Jetfires. The turbo engine also proved to be troublesome, which obviously didn't help sales. Despite heavy promotion, the Jetfire tallied only 5842 deliveries for '63. Predictably, it did not return in the bulkier, restyled '64 Cutlass line.

These '64s were exactly what the public seemed to want, however: longer, wider, and heavier. The

The unique Cutlass Jetfire was in its second and final year for 1963, and bore the more important-looking outer skin redo applied to all of Oldsmobile's compacts that year. Rear fender insignia emphasizes this model's exclusive turbocharged V-8. Handsomely furnished cabin is dominated by the simple instrument panel adorned with the Jetfire name in the center. Note shifter console with turbo boost gauge. (Owner: John Pirochta)

The '63 Jetfire's brushed-finish bodyside trim and its squared-off rear deck owed quite a lot to the full-size Starfire, but there was nothing like the Turbo Rocket V-8 anywhere else in the division's stable. The efficient, lightweight powerplant put out 1 bhp for each of its 215 cubic inches and could propel the Jetfire from rest to 60 mph in about 8.5 seconds. Unfortunately, it was less reliable than more conventional V-8s, which contributed to the Jetfire's early demise. (Owner: John Pirochta)

sophisticated Jetfire V-8 was dumped in favor of an ordinary 400-cid V-8 for a new performance compact dubbed 4-4-2. It wasn't as efficient with a gallon of gasoline, but its sales success reinforced Detroit dogma that would go unchallenged for years to come: there's no substitute for cubic inches.

Actually there was a substitute, and it performed quite nicely. And if it didn't seem necessary or even all that appealing in 1963, it certainly does today. A Jetfire now commands far more money

in collectors circles than a non-turbo '63 Cutlass or even a 326 Tempest. So many cars are *wrong* for their time. The Jetfire was in that small group of automobiles that were simply *ahead* of their time.

Parts are scarce today, so if you're lucky enough to find a Jetfire, consider joining the Oldsmobile Club of America (P.O. Box 16216, Lansing MI 48901). Even better, you'll meet others who haven't forgotten about Oldsmobile's only turbocharged car.

OLDSMOBILE TORONADO 1966

The most talked-about new car of 1966 was the front-wheel drive Oldsmobile Toronado. It was America's first attempt at front drive since the classic Cord 810/812 of 1936–37, and it was far more successful. The Toronado even looked a bit like the Cord, with its burly styled steel wheels, louvered grille, and prominent fender outlines. Everything about the Toro, from its imposing size to its huge 425-cid V-8, suggested power, prestige, and excitement.

Toronado shared its basic body structure, but not sheetmetal, with the second-generation Buick Riviera that also debuted for '66. But while Riviera had conventional rear drive and quite

orthodox styling, the Toronado was decidedly different, and Oldsmobile made the most of it. Here was the sort of innovation we had come to expect from the outfit that had introduced the automatic transmission in 1938 and the overhead-valve V-8 in 1949.

Naturally, this newest Olds was showered with attention. *Motor Trend* magazine named it Car of the Year and recorded impressive performance figures: 9.5 seconds in the 0-60 mph dash and 17 seconds in the standing-start quarter-mile at a trap speed of 82 mph. In a prescient new-model assessment, *MT*'s editors declared: "The Toronado's a truly outstanding car, and this first model is highly perfected.

We think it's destined to become a classic in its own time." Other enthusiast publications were equally impressed. The Toronado walked away with *Car Life*'s engineering excellence award and was voted best luxury and personal car by the readers of *Car and Driver*.

Detroit measures success on the sales charts, however, and the premiere Toronado was an unqualified winner here, too. Model year sales

An imposing front end with considerable front overhang emphasized the '66 Toronado's novel front-wheel drive. (Owner: Ken Nelson)

reached 40,963, far behind Thunderbird but close to Riviera's total. With prices starting at $4585, the base Toro was a relative bargain in its market segment. Standard equipment included front and rear seat belts, full carpeting, electric clock, two-speed windshield wipers with washers, backup lamps, a courtesy light package, and six-passenger seating via a full-width front bench. To this, the deluxe model added a bucket-style "Strato" front seat with pull-down center armrest, chrome interior moldings for windshield and windows, and wheel trim rings.

Of course, the Toronado's most interesting aspect was that driveline. The standard and only available transmission was a special "split" version of GM's Turbo Hydra-Matic, with the torque converter directly behind the

engine and the gearbox mounted under the left-side cylinder bank. Connecting them was a two-inch multiple-link chain. Differential torque was split evenly between the halfshafts. For a new design, the Toronado was surprisingly trouble-free, thanks to an extensive pre-production testing program. The drum brakes were a weak spot, however, and front tires wore quickly because of the front-heavy weight

distribution and the additional burden of being the driven as well as the steered wheels. Radial tires and front disc brakes were added as options for 1967 to alleviate these deficiencies.

Toronado was born in an age when big was assumed to be better, and its dimensions were impressive. Overall length was 211 inches, wheelbase was 119 inches, and approximate curb weight was a hefty 4500 pounds.

Besides its front-drive engineering, the 1966 Toronado broke fresh ground in styling with an unbroken C-pillar line, handsomely flared wheel openings, and deftly handled proportions that belied its big-car 119-inch wheelbase. Hidden headlamps, louvered grille, and slotted wheels echoed the design of its front-drive Cord 810/812 predecessor. (Both cars owned by Ken Nelson)

Thanks to the flat-floor interior made possible by front drive, passenger room was quite good compared to the personal-luxury competition.

Like virtually every American car of the Sixties, the Toronado could be personalized via a lengthy list of options. Popular extras included AM/FM radio, tilt/telescope steering wheel, power windows, tinted glass, air conditioning, and power decklid release. In-

teriors were available in seven colors, and materials included cloth, vinyl or leather.

Toronado's big splash and good debut-year sales delighted division management, but the initial success wore off quickly. Sales of the little-changed '67s slumped sharply, as Oldsmobile discovered that mechanical innovation alone was not enough to sway would-be Thunderbird buyers. Also, Cadillac introduced its conventional-looking Eldorado that year, which shared the same front-drive mechanicals but swept past the Toro in sales volume by virtue of luxury appointments and a prestigious name. As the Sixties progressed, Toronado styling was progressively watered down to suit mainstream tastes. By 1971 the car was almost devoid of character, its front-wheel drive system retained almost as an afterthought. But sales went up, and early Toros became back-lot specials.

Values on first-generation Toronados (1966–70) remained depressed for a long time, thanks to the car's healthy appetite for fuel and the high cost of spare parts. But that situation is changing. The Toro is still a bargain, but collectors now realize its historic significance. Buy one now, because they won't be cheap for long.

PLYMOUTH
SPORT FURY 1964

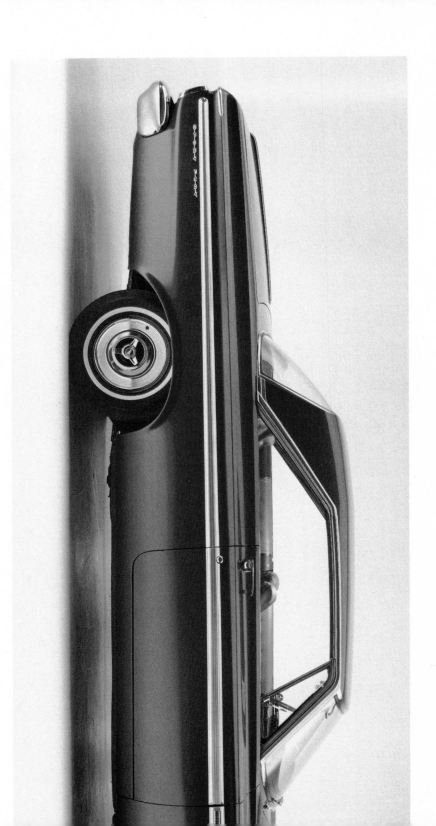

Plymouth recovered strongly from its early-Sixties doldrums with a sharp new car line for 1964. Chrysler's volume division delivered almost 600,000 cars during the model year, and the standard-sized Plymouth led the sales charge.

On a 116-inch wheelbase and measuring 205 inches overall, the "full-size" Plymouth for '64 was sized between the standard Chevrolet and the new intermediate Chevelle. Plymouth owners might have called it a "happy medium" kind of car. It didn't compare inch-for-inch with the standard Ford or Chevy, but in many ways it more than measured up.

Police departments and taxi companies may have favored the cheapie Savoy models, but the mid-range Belvedere was unquestionably a more civilized choice for non-fleet buyers. Every successful Sixties automaker needed an Impala kind of car, and the

Fury continued as Plymouth's entry in the low-cost luxury field. The top-line series was available in a full range of body styles: sedans, wagons, hardtops, and a convertible. This year's ultimate Plymouth was still the Sport Fury, offered in hardtop coupe and convertible form with prices starting at just $2864.

Although the 1964 Plymouths were largely unchanged under the surface from their 1962–63 predecessors, styling was thoroughly updated with a Chevy-like grille, a faster-looking two-door hardtop roofline, and revised side trim. The contours were bulkier overall, but somehow the restyle suggested better performance. Sport Fury exclusives included discreet red, white, and blue side decoration and special wheel covers with simulated knock-off hubs. Every '64 Plymouth came with an alternator, torsion-bar front suspension, and fully unitized construction.

And Plymouth was still the only one of the "low-priced three" to offer a 5-year/50,000-mile warranty.

Though lesser Plymouths had Chrysler Corporation's respected 225-cid Slant Six as their standard powerplant, the Sport Fury received a 230-bhp 318-cid V-8. Several other V-8s were offered optionally: a 265-bhp 361, a 305-bhp 383, and a 365-bhp 426 wedge. There were also "SuperStock" versions that put out either 415 or 425 bhp depending on tune. The fabulous 426 Hemi was introduced early in 1964, but for race-car use only. Chrysler wouldn't release a street version until 1966. Nevertheless, Plymouth's '64 engine selection was at least a match for anything Ford or Chevy had to offer.

Plymouth's 3-speed TorqueFlite automatic transmission was a family favorite, and its tough-as-nails build and positive shift action made it

Plymouth was in the third year of a three-year styling cycle for 1964, adopting a more Chevy-like appearance that removed the last vestiges of Virgil Exner's curious original design for '62. The Sport Fury hardtop coupe shared a new V-shaped rear roofline with its lower-price siblings, but retained distinctive side trim. (Chrysler Historical Collection)

popular with drag racers too. No other automatic could match TorqueFlite in the quarter-mile. As with other Chrysler makes, Plymouth used pushbutton gear selection for the last time on its '64 TorqueFlite models. A 3-speed manual was standard, and a 4-speed with Hurst shifter was optional on all Sport Furys.

Good looks, improving quality, and that comprehensive warranty all contributed to Plymouth's sales success in '64. Other factors included a wide selection of performance options, excellent road manners, and competitive prices. The Sport Fury shared in the growth by almost doubling its 1963 sales total, convertible production reaching 3858 and the hardtop coupe finding 23,695 buyers.

Though Plymouth had seen improved sales since 1962, it still needed a traditional full-size model of the sort it had not fielded for three years. Accordingly, the Fury was an entirely new car for 1965, resting on a large 119-inch wheelbase, the same as that of this year's completely redone big Ford and Chevrolet. What had been the standard Plymouth became the intermediate Belvedere/Satellite, and that's where the performance emphasis shifted. Thus, the 1964 was the last "hot" Sport Fury, and it's one col-

lectors seek out today for its fine handling, responsive performance, and lively looks. These cars are still bargain-priced, and only a super-sharp convertible or 426 hardtop is likely to bring anything over $5000. Compare that with modern econo-tin. Adding to the '64 Sport Fury's appeal is the low number of survivors, which is why you see so few offered for sale.

Driving the '64 Sport Fury is an experience to savor. The steering is light and precise, and the handling is good even by today's standards. The original-equipment tires were the weak link, but the torsion-bar suspension

strikes a fine balance between comfort and roadability, unlike those of too many of today's "muscle cars." Gas mileage is surprisingly good with the 318, and acceleration is quite brisk. If you're lucky enough to locate one of the rare 383 or 426 cars, don't expect much in the way of fuel economy. Do expect lots of go.

Perhaps the best thing about owning an early-Sixties Plymouth is knowing that it's barely broken-in at 100,000 miles. It was the kind of near-bullet-proof machine that made Detroit the envy of the automotive world at the time. Come to think of it, it still does.

PLYMOUTH
ROAD RUNNER 1968

The Plymouth Road Runner was one of those cars that came around at exactly the right time. Pontiac's original GTO had been followed by a hoard of muscle machines in the mid-Sixties, but by 1968 they had become increasingly flabby, complacent, and costly. The Road Runner, on the other hand, was quick, spartan, and cheap. It also had an endearing, unique touch of whimsy: a horn that went "beep-beep" just like its cartoon namesake.

Plymouth's more traditional supercar in these years was the GTX, which had been introduced for 1967. Like all Chrysler Corporation intermediates, the '68 version was pleasantly restyled,

with curvier contours and a softer roofline. Motivating force was provided by a brawny "Super Commando" 440-cid V-8 flexing 375-bhp worth of muscle. Other equipment included cushy bucket seats, simulated wood trim, stripes, and lots of chrome. The base price of the GTX's velvet-lined brawn was $3329 in hardtop

coupe form (the convertible cost even more), and that was too high for the sort of younger but less well-heeled buyers likely to want it.

Enter the Road Runner. Introduced on September 14, 1967, it was essentially a GTX without the fluff and pegged at $2870 basic. For that money you got a basic Belvedere pillared coupe (Plymouth's lightest mid-size body style, a fact drag racers were quick to note) with a plain cloth-and-vinyl bench-seat interior, a minimum of exterior ornamentation, and a hairy 383-cid V-8 under a special hood. This engine was dressed with high-performance heads, a wilder cam, four-barrel carburetor, and dual exhausts. Horsepower was 335 at 5200 rpm. The only

engine option was the legendary "King Kong," the 426-cid Hemi, priced at $714 and thus not frequently ordered. If the Runner was a bit undertrimmed above, it was fully equipped underneath. The chassis was beefed-up via heavy-duty 11-inch drum brakes, F70 × 14 red- or whiteline tires, a stabilizer bar, and heavy-duty torsion bars, springs, and shocks. A 4-speed manual transmission was standard, and the proven 3-speed TorqueFlite automatic cost a paltry $38.95 extra.

The Road Runner caught on like crazy, and at the same time made some other muscle cars look a bit silly. Suddenly, performance magazines were pointing out that vinyl tops,

bucket seats, and other comfy-cruiser add-ons meant worse, not better, elapsed times. By mid-1968 the Runner had clearly supplanted the GTX as Plymouth's main entry in the supercar sweepstakes, so the marketing department decided to broaden the concept's appeal by fielding a hardtop coupe version and adding new interior trims and even a—gulp!—vinyl roof. It's almost amazing that the original successful formula was already being watered down. The hardtop came in at around $3000, and with the luxury trim it came close to GTX price territory.

The Plymouth Road Runner hardtop from mid-1968. (Chrysler Historical Collection)

When all the votes had been cast, Road Runner sales topped 44,000 for the 1968 model year, split between 29,240 pillared coupes and 15,357 two-door hardtops. This naturally hurt the GTX, which scored only 18,940 sales. The Runner had proven itself as street-wise, while the alphabet model just wasn't cutting it in the executive hot-rod league.

The competition was nearly as quick as Plymouth itself to capitalize on the Road Runner phenomenon. Dodge had a bargain-priced Coronet Super Bee in its showrooms by February 1968, and the 1969 model year brought a stripped version of the Chevelle SS396 from Chevrolet and a bargain-basement Torino Cobra from Ford. At mid-year, the flamboyant Pontiac GTO Judge appeared, as the original muscle car was forced to play catch-up.

Motor Trend magazine recognized the importance of the low-cost performance phenomenon by naming Road Runner Car of the Year in February 1969. The Runner proliferated this year with the addition of a convertible. The ragtop was not popular, although it's a much-treasured collectible today.

Sales of all supercars declined for model year 1970, thanks to pressure from insurance companies and the government. Ironically, the Runner was injured further by the success of an even cheaper muscle machine within the Plymouth line, the compact Duster 340. It was everything the '68 Runner had been, except it was fashionably smaller and had a horn that didn't go "beep-beep."

The 1971 Runner was bigger, more expensive, and didn't go as fast. More of the same for 1972 and 1973 meant more sales declines. Ultimately, the Road Runner was reduced to a mere "paint-on performance" package for the late-Seventies Volare.

The '68 Road Runner was a Detroit muscle car, pure and simple. It didn't have stripes or spoilers, but it more than delivered on its performance promises. Such was the real beauty of the fast 'n frill-less coupe that all too briefly ran away with the imagination of America's youth. Beep-beep!

America's first "budget" muscle car debuted as a fixed-pillar coupe with minimal exterior ornamentation and a no-frills interior. The heart of the package was the 383-cid Super Commando V-8 with 335 bhp, plus a "beep-beep" horn. (Chrysler Historical Collection)

PONTIAC CATALINA 1960

If any make can be said to have owned the Sixties, it would have to be Pontiac. Throughout the decade, Pontiac outsold every other medium-priced rival with a satisfying combination of horsepower, style, and especially value. The Pontiacs of these years were priced only a little higher than comparable Fords and Chevys, and offered discernably more in the way of luxury and performance features.

Pontiac's renaissance began with its 1959 "Wide-Track" models. That year saw the division field its biggest V-8

yet, the "Trophy" 389, and a new series that would become increasingly popular with value- and performance-conscious motorists in the Sixties. Its name was Catalina. After a highly successful season, most observers expected Pontiac to rest on its laurels a bit for 1960, but it didn't. Though they weren't new from the ground up, these cars did have new styling, new options, more luxury, and another new nameplate.

The facelifted 1960 Pontiac was announced by a clean, horizontal grille, replacing the distinctive '59 twin-oval

affair. The new nose was attractive, but the split grille had become something of a Pontiac trademark in just that one year, so it returned for 1961. It's been with us ever since. Other, less controversial aspects of the revised 1960 styling included simple, elegant bodyside ornamentation, a crisply tailored rear deck with four high-set

Pontiac's extra-cost aluminum wheel and hub assemblies dressed up even the 1960 Catalina convertible, which was already plenty stylish. (Owner: Dan Mamsen)

taillights, and glassy superstructures retained from 1959.

The handsomely crafted Bonneville series remained the most prestigious Pontiac for 1960, available as a hardtop coupe, hardtop sedan, four-door wagon, and convertible. All models rode a princely 124-inch wheelbase and came with such royal touches as a padded instrument panel trimmed in polished walnut, a rich fabric/vinyl interior, and a gold-plated *Bonneville* grille ornament. A 303-bhp four-barrel version of the 389 was standard for all models. The most desirable Bonneville was, of course, the exciting convertible, featuring a genuine leather interior and optional front bucket seats.

Next step down on the Pontiac ladder was the Star Chief. Resting on the same 124-inch wheelbase as the Bonneville, it was available as a four-door sedan and four-door hardtop only, and it appealed to a diminishing number of Pontiac buyers who valued tradition. The Star Chief no longer bore Silver Streaks, a straight eight, and top-of-the-line status, and it was as conservative as Pontiac got for 1960.

The big news this year was the Ventura, a Catalina with the custom touch and sharing its shorter 122-inch wheelbase. Highlights included a plush all-vinyl interior, full carpeting, a custom steering wheel, and full wheel covers. The only body styles available were two- and four-door hardtops.

For all that a Pontiac dealer had to offer, the overwhelming popularity champ was the low-priced Catalina series, which comprised two- and four-door sedans, two- and four-door hardtops, a convertible, and six- and nine-passenger station wagons. Prices started as low as $2702, and the impressive list of standard equipment ran to a choice of 15 body colors, five interior hues, full carpeting, electric wipers, cigarette lighter, front and rear armrests, and a foam-cushion front seat. A premium-fuel 389 V-8 rated at 283 bhp was standard, but buyers could choose a regular-gas 215-bhp version at no extra charge. A 3-speed column-shift transmission was basic.

Pontiac's facelift on its one-year-old '59 design was fairly extensive even for 1960. The most noticeable alterations were the new full-width horizontal-bar grille and a reworked rear end with the taillamps carried up high in the trailing edges of the fenders instead of in the back panel. This lovingly restored Catalina convertible sports a number of optional extras from the wide selection originally offered, including radio, heater/defroster, automatic, whitewalls, and twin fender mirrors, in addition to the special aluminum wheels and hubs. (Owner: Dan Mamsen)

Top: Pontiac built exactly 17,172 of its 1960 Catalina convertibles. Only the nine-passenger Safari wagon saw fewer deliveries in this series this year. The ragtop's base list price was a reasonable $3078. Above: A big car built on a long 122-inch wheelbase, the 1960 Catalina convertible offered plenty of room for four, though back seat space was necessarily more limited than in other body styles due to the space-robbing well for the convertible top. Right: Beautiful aluminum wheel/hub assemblies added to the performance image of the early "Wide-Track" Pontiacs. (Owner: Dan Mamsen.)

Few automakers in the Sixties offered more optional equipment and accessories than Pontiac, so any Catalina could be tailored exactly to the purchaser's specifications. Many were. Major options included air conditioning, "Magi-Cruise" speed control, "Safe-T-Track" limited-slip differential, tinted glass, and power seats, brakes, and windows. Even the heater and defroster were optional. Other available equipment included dual exhausts, whitewalls, a remote-control outside mirror, spotlight, and seat belts. An electric clock was optional on Catalinas but standard on other '60 Pontiacs.

Properly equipped, the light Catalina coupe could be a very hot car. The proper equipment might include the 318-bhp 389 with Tri Power (triple two-barrel carbs), a close-ratio manual transmission or the Hydra-Matic, Safe-T-Track, Pontiac's beautiful new aluminum wheel and drum assemblies, and a full-flow oil filter. Showboaters would have ordered much the same, but might have put it on a Ventura hardtop coupe and added whitewalls, power steering, and possibly the new "Sportable" transistor radio.

Racing honed an already sharp performance image that Pontiac had established by 1960. It was America's finest popularly priced "road car." A Chrysler 300 was faster, but it wasn't as affordable. A Chevrolet was cheaper, but it was hard-pressed to match Pontiac's combination of speed and style. The public obviously liked that combination, because it scooped up an impressive 396,716 of the 1960 models. With its limited model line and "old folks" image, Star Chief accounted for only 43,691 sales, including just 166 with the standard 3-speed manual transmission. The Ventura snagged 56,277 customers in its first year, and the prestigious Bonneville corralled another 85,277. The Catalina was the overwhelming favorite way to go "Wide-Tracking," the model year total standing at 210,934.

Value did not go unrecognized, and the Pontiac that could be made to order was exactly the kind of car America admired in 1960. Come to that, this Catalina is still admired today, and remains one of the lesser-known but still great cars of the Sixties.

PONTIAC GTO 1966

With 389 cubic inches of V-8 engine stuffed into a lightweight intermediate body, the Pontiac GTO quickly became an American high-performance legend. It still is. The 1966 edition was the most popular of all, sales reaching 96,946 for the first and only time.

A performance option for the workaday LeMans coupe, convertible, and two-door hardtop in 1964-65, the GTO became a series unto itself for '66 and featured even more distinctive styling. The design wasn't all-new, but it

looked it. Curves replaced angles, a "flying buttress" rear window treatment inspired a host of imitators, and the traditional split grille and vertically stacked headlamps were a reminder to would-be competitors that GTO intended to stay on top of the suddenly competitive muscle-car heap. Body styles remained as before.

Prices started at just $2783 for the pillared coupe, the body style much favored by serious racers for its lighter weight and greater structural rigidity. Production was 10,363 units. Most

non-racing buyers preferred the sleek hardtop, priced at $2847 basic. Sales totaled 73,785. The convertible was the heaviest and most expensive '66 GTO, but it tallied a respectable 12,798 deliveries for the model year.

Standard GTO equipment for '66 included "Strato" front bucket seats, a wood-trimmed padded instrument panel, carpeting, full-foam seat construction, exterior pinstriping, hood

The Pontiac GTO hardtop coupe for 1966 sold at $2847 base. (Owner: Chris Terry)

scoop, and a power top for the convertible. Available exterior colors numbered 16, and all-vinyl interiors were offered in blue, turquoise, bronze, red, black, or parchment. A vinyl roof covering, introduced in mid-1965, remained an option for closed models. Other dress-up items included a full range of wheel covers and styled road wheels, red plastic fender liners (new this year and rare today), center console, and a steering wheel with simulated wood rim. Headrests were optional, and the available walnut shift knob added a classy touch. For the safety-minded, front and rear seat lap belts, outside rear view mirror, padded dash and sunvisors, and a stronger windshield were standard equipment on all 1966 General Motors cars.

The GTO's standard engine was still the 389-cid V-8 that had been powering Pontiacs since 1959. Rated at 335 bhp for '66, it was trimmed with chrome rocker covers, low-restriction air cleaner, and oil filler cap. A front stabilizer and heavy-duty clutch, shocks, and springs were also part of the package. Pontiac was aware that its cars were being driven with some "enthusiasm" on the street, hence the rugged components. The "cooking" 389 was plenty hot, but it was positively torrid when fitted with triple two-barrel carbs, which bumped horsepower to a sizzling 360. A Ram-Air package was also offered during the model year, which upped output by an undisclosed amount. In response to the safety establishment's renewed criticism of high-performance cars, the tri-carb set-up was dropped in mid-1966, making GTOs so-equipped valuable collectibles. As before, the standard transmission was an all-synchro 3-speed with column-mount shifter, but most customers preferred the optional 4-speed manual with Hurst floorshift. Automatic was also available, and found 35,667 buyers. All these shifters could be housed in an optional chrome center console. Other extras included exhaust splitters, tilt steering wheel, tachometer, transistorized ignition, AM/FM radio, and air conditioning.

When fast cars gathered in the mid-1960s, the one to beat was usually a GTO, or "Goat" as it was nicknamed on the street. Others, including Pontiac, called it the "Tiger," and rival makes could only wish their mid-size muscle machines matched the GTO

GM intermediates got new, smoother body lines for 1966, and the Pontiac GTO was perhaps the cleanest-looking of the bunch. Highlights included "tunnel" backlight treatment, "Coke-bottle" rear fenders, and stacked quad headlamps. Beefy 389 V-8 put out up to 360 bhp in optional tune. Red inner fender liners were a new accessory this year, but rarely ordered. (Owner: Chris Terry)

for image and impact. There were certainly plenty of competitors in 1966, such as the Chevelle SS396, hot new "street Hemis" in intermediates from Plymouth and Dodge, the Olds 4-4-2, and a high-

performance Fairlane from Ford. GTO added weight, gained inches, and offered luxury equipment unheard of only two years earlier, but that was the price of success in '66. More GTOs were sold to boulevard cruisers than Buick Skylark Gran Sport, and a high-

street racers, though the car was considered a first-class ride by either group. Then sales began a steady and prolonged decline. The last GTO had all the character of a Chevy Nova, which in fact it was. The real killer was the hostility of the nation's insurance companies, which collectively succeeded in smothering performance cars with prohibitive rates. By 1970, people who wanted truly exciting cars just couldn't afford to buy them anymore.

All of which makes 1966 the year that marked GTO at its peak. It was pretty, fast, and affordable. In short, it was the tiger that every red-blooded American youngster wanted, "The Great One" then and now. GRRRRRR!

PONTIAC 2+2 1967

Sometimes even Pontiac buffs forget that The Great One had a big brother. But anyone who's ever buckled into the bucket seat of a Catalina 2+2 knows that Pontiac built more than one kind of performance machine in the Sixties. The 1967 model showcased on these pages was one of the last of a muscular breed. Today the 2+2 is a car that collectors are only beginning to appreciate.

The Wide-Track people had been building hot full-size cars long before '67, of course. Tri-Power Venturas were among the quickest street machines in 1960-61, the late Fireball Roberts drove more than one '62 Catalina down NASCAR's victory lanes, and the 1963 Super-Duty 421 Catalina was a seldom seen but greatly feared quarter-mile competitor. The 1964 Catalina 2+2 was the bucket-seat

production successor to those revered Pontiacs. It was also the division's challenge to the likes of Chevy's Impala Super Sport and Ford's Galaxie 500/XL. Unlike so many of its competitors, the 2+2 was more than a trim package. In addition to the obligatory front bucket seats, this enthusiast-oriented option group for the Catalina two-door hardtop comprised a heavy-duty suspension and a no-nonsense

Though still based on the new-for-'65 bodyshell, the full-size 1967 Pontiacs gained styling distinction via "hippier" rear fenderlines and a massive new bumper/grille with a more prominent central "beak." Catalina 2 + 2 was identified only by simulated louvers on the front fenders and small badges. (Pontiac Motor Division)

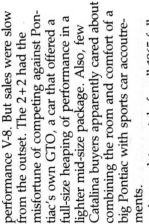

performance V-8. But sales were slow from the outset. The 2+2 had the misfortune of competing against Pontiac's own GTO, a car that offered a full-size heaping of performance in a lighter mid-size package. Also, few Catalina buyers apparently cared about combining the room and comfort of a big Pontiac with sports car accoutrements.

A complete restyle for all 1965 full-size Pontiacs endowed the 2+2 with a sharp new look, highlighted by shapely rear fenders and a "faster" roofline. Changes were minimal for 1966, but the '67 was draped in new, more daring sheetmetal. Chassis

design and inner body structure was unchanged, but GM's much-favored "coke-bottle" look was carried to a new extreme. A bulging rear fender line and true fastback styling were central to the new design, as were an integral bumper/grille and "disappearing" windshield wipers."

New options for '67 included a hood-mounted tachometer (no kidding!) and front shoulder belts. Standard safety features fitted to all Pontiacs this year were lap belts, an "energy-absorbing" steering column and wheel, padded instrument panel, four-way hazard warning flasher, backup lights, and dual-speed windshield wipers. Of far more interest to performance fans was a new 428-cid V-8 that served up 360 capable horsepower. If you needed more than that, Pontiac had it in a 376-bhp premium-fuel Quadra-Power 428, with 10.75:1 compression, optional at extra cost. A floor-mounted 3-speed transmission, bucket seats, and a special suspension were standard on every 2+2. The option list could make things even

more interesting, with such items as Pontiac's beautiful aluminum wheel/drum assemblies, a 4-speed manual or Turbo Hydra-Matic transmission, axle ratios for every driving requirement, even a heavy-duty frame (standard on convertibles). Luxury lovers could order their Wide-Track with air conditioning, stereo, tinted glass, cruise control, and power windows.

Sadly, not many 2+2s of any kind were ordered in 1967. Even though prices started at just $3360, production reached only 1768 units before Pontiac pulled the plug. You could still order the 2+2's performance equipment on a '68 Ventura by checking the right options on the order form, but few did. By 1969, the full-size performance Pontiac was history, though the hotter versions of that year's completely revamped Grand Prix made a highly satisfying substitute.

And it's low production numbers that make that brutal, beautiful 2+2 a rare find today. If only car buffs had paid attention long before 1984, we might be seeing more of "Big Brother" now.

PONTIAC FIREBIRD 1969

Firebird moved closer to being an all-Pontiac ponycar for 1969. The 1967-68 models were pretty but very Camaro-like. This year, however, Firebird had an aggressive new look all its own—and new muscle to back it up.

Even though an all-new second-generation Camaro/Firebird was waiting in the wings for 1970 introduction, the '69s were restyled to a surprising degree. Firebird sheetmetal was almost all new, and the result was a heavier-looking car with a definite GTO character. The new grille was controversial but practical, the protruding snout wrapped with Endura energy-absorbing plastic and doubling as the bumper. This was the last year

for several Firebird options, models, and packages popular with enthusiast-minded motorists, including the lovely Firebird convertible, the exclusive Pontiac overhead-camshaft six-cylinder engine, and the unique hood-mounted tachometer. The hood tach wasn't missed much, but car lovers did mourn for the other two.

But 1969 was also a year of Firebird firsts. In particular, it brought the premiere of the Trans Am, a model that would become a Pontiac legend in ensuing years. In '69, though, it was simply a mid-year addition aimed at the competition crowd and something most buyers had never heard of. Inspired by the racing Firebirds running

in the SCCA's Trans-Am sedan series, the street T/A was introduced along with the GTO Judge at that year's Chicago Auto Show. The only color scheme available was solid white with contrasting blue hood, roof, and deck striping. Equipment included a Ram-Air 400 V-8 rated at 335 bhp, a heavy-duty 3-speed manual transmission, special handling package, variable-ratio power steering, padded-rim steering wheel, functional front fender air extractors, and a modest air spoiler on the trunklid. Options included 4-speed manual transmission, Turbo Hydra-Matic, and the division's Ram-Air IV V-8, along with the standard Firebird's lengthy list of comfort/convenience

add-ons. Only 697 Trans Ams were built for the '69 model year, including just eight convertibles.

Regular Firebirds could be ordered in five forms: the base, the six-cylinder Sprint, the 350, the H.O., and the magnificent 400. Buyers on a budget flocked to the base model, priced from $2830 and offering features other ponycars couldn't match at any price. Foremost among them was Pontiac's high-revving overhead-cam six, rated at 175 bhp in standard tune. Other no-cost items were E70-14 tires, front bucket seats, cabin carpeting, and "Space Saver" spare tire. For $214 more, you could get all this and a convertible top too.

Next up the Firebird pecking order was a car truly unusual for late-Sixties Detroit. Dubbed Firebird Sprint, it came with racing stripes, a sport suspension, and a four-barrel version of the "cammer" six, rated at a remarkable 215 bhp. Contemporary

road testers found it a delightfully responsive car on the open road, especially when equipped with the optional 4-speed transmission.

Firebird's volume leader for '69 was the far more conventional 350. Equipment included a 265-bhp regular-fuel 350-cid V-8 and F70 × 14 tires. Of

The 1969 Pontiac Firebird shared a heavy outer sheetmetal revamp with this year's Chevrolet Camaro, but was more obviously different thanks to a prominent split bumper/grille, more front overhang, and a different back panel treatment. Shown here is the hot Firebird 400 convertible. (Owner: Mike Abbott)

Above: The '69 Firebird 400 was named for its engine measurement in cubic inches. Big-block V-8 was rated at an easy 330 bhp in standard form, with up to 345 bhp available with optional Ram Air induction. Right: Hood-mounted tachometer was an exclusive Pontiac optional gimmick for '69, and it proved relatively practical. Below: Slim "slat" taillamps were an identifying Pontiac styling feature of the late Sixties. (Owner: Mike Abbott)

more interest to collectors was the next model up the line, the 350 H.O. With this package you got a hot 325-bhp premium-fuel four-barrel 350, heavy-duty 3-speed manual gearbox, heavy-duty battery, and dual exhausts.

For those who considered cubic inches the only answer to their performance needs, Pontiac had the Firebird 400. This was the muscle-bound set-up that went best with the beefy new body build. Red- or white-stripe wide-oval tires, hood scoops, special handling suspension, chrome engine dress-up kit, and dual exhausts were yours without asking, along with a 400-cid V-8 rated at 330 bhp. Two Ram-Air engines, offering 335 and 345 bhp, were optional. Other popular extra-cost items included Rally II wheels, tilt steering wheel, and single-piston power front disc brakes.

Interior styling on all 1969 Firebirds was slightly revised, with a fresh instrument panel facing, a new standard steering wheel, and new seat trims. An all-leather bucket-seat interior, available only in Antique Gold, was a new option. There were 15 exterior colors available, and hardtops could be ordered with a vinyl top in any one of six shades. Convertible tops were done in black, white, ivory, dark blue, and dark green.

This Firebird was more ponycar than Pontiac had ever offered, yet sales were disappointing. Model year production fell from 107,112 units for 1968 to 87,011. It wasn't the car's fault, although the new front end may have sent a few prospects looking at Camaros. The market had simply turned towards economy, and Firebird was anything but an economy car. Only 20,893 of the '69s were equipped with the ohc six, an engine Pontiac had promoted as a performance unit, not a mileage-maker. Although that figure was up from the 1968 total, it wasn't enough to stem the overall decline. Interestingly, when the all-new '70 Firebird debuted, it carried the uninspiring Chevrolet pushrod six as standard equipment, and only 3134 cars were built with that engine for the abbreviated model year.

Today's collectors recognize the 1969 models as the last, and perhaps the best, of the very special first-generation Firebird. From Sprint to Trans Am, from H.O. hardtop to 400 convertible, they were all goin' machines—and among the great cars of the Sixties.

STUDEBAKER
HAWK GT 1962

Studebaker struggled for survival in the Sixties. It lost that struggle, but not before it had produced a number of interesting cars that are now much desired. The elegant machine you see on these pages is a 1962 Studebaker Hawk GT, a car that would have succeeded under another nameplate. Nobody wants to buy an orphan, however, and in 1962 that was just the situation facing Studebaker. America's oldest surviving automaker had arrived at one of its periodic low ebbs in 1961, but this time

it wouldn't be able to recover. An economic recession had devastated the South Bend firm's sales, and there was now very little money in the company's coffers to develop badly needed new products. Studebaker president Sherwood Egbert called in noted industrial designer Brooks Stevens to modernize the aging Lark and the equally antiquated Hawk coupe. It was a desperate move made at the last minute, so Stevens was given pretty much carte blanche. The result was a successfully updated com-

pact for 1962-63 and an even more successful new personal-luxury car. The Hawk began life as a 1956 reformulation of the brilliantly styled 1953-54 "Loewy coupe." Designed principally by Bob Bourke of Studebaker Styling, the Hawk was marked by fins and a square grille, and by '61 it looked decidedly old. Detroit would have thrown away such an outmoded

The Studebaker Gran Turismo Hawk for 1962. (Owners: Larry and Sandra Van Horn)

car, but Studebaker couldn't afford that. Told to do what he could with it, Stevens took one look and saw potential. He shaved off the fins, added a Thunderbird-like roofline (which was very popular with every automaker by the early Sixties), cleaned up the detail debris, and installed a new instrument panel with curved cluster full of round, legible gauges, unusual in gadget-ridden 1962.

The end product caught auto writers and industry sleuths off guard. Nobody expected a new Hawk for '62, let alone such a handsome one. Even competitive designers admitted the job was masterful, especially considering Stevens' severe budget limitations. Christened Gran Turismo Hawk, the new car did show its '53 parentage, but only if you looked closely.

The born-again Hawk wasn't just a "looker." It was a mover too. A 210-bhp 289 V-8 was standard, and an optional 225-bhp "Thunderbolt" version was available to put the lighter Hawk ahead of Thunderbird in the performance department. A 3-speed manual gearbox was standard, but automatic, an overdrive 3-speed, and a Borg-Warner 4-speed manual could be specified. Enthusiast magazines were impressed by the GT Hawk's abilities. *Motor Trend* magazine timed a 210-bhp car from 0-60 mph in 11.7 seconds, and judged it "a willing and able car definitely in the tradition of the high-speed tourers of Europe." This good go was augmented by good show: comfortable all-vinyl bucket seats, walnut-grained dash, fold-down rear armrest, and color-keyed interior trim. With a base price of $3095, the GT Hawk was more than competitive, and a long list of options could turn it into a very personal car indeed. The extras included sunroof, power windows, air conditioning, power steering, air conditioning, Twin-Traction limited-slip differential, decklid radio antenna, and tachometer.

The market for sports-personal cars was exploding in the early Sixties, and the deftly styled Hawk beat the Buick Riviera to market by a full year. With its low price, high style, and ample go-power, the GT Hawk couldn't miss. But it did. Although sales rose from a miserable 3340 of the finned '61s to 8388 GTs, it was a drop in the bucket when Chevrolet was selling 200,000 Corvair Monzas and Ford was retailing 70,000 Thunderbirds that same season. And, of course, this was hardly

enough volume to spark a renaissance for Studebaker as a whole.

There was a 1963 GT Hawk but, sadly, sales slumped to 4634. The '64 version was the best yet, but only 1767 were called for. When Studebaker consolidated production at its Hamilton, Ontario plant for one last stand in the

auto business, the Hawk didn't go along. There was no point.

Those who feared being stuck with an "orphan" car missed out on a very good thing. Today, the GT Hawk remains a stunning Studebaker that's all too rarely seen, but a great car of the Sixties.

Brooks Stevens' styling surgery on the 10-year-old "Loewy coupe" bodyshell was startlingly effective, one reason why the Studebaker GT Hawk has become a collector's item today. Clean flanks, a Thunderbird-like roofline, and a tastefully revamped rear deck are the major changes highlighted here. Studebaker's venerable 289-cid V-8 was the sole powerplant available. (Owners: Larry and Sandra Van Horn)

STUDEBAKER AVANTI 1963

I f any car of the Sixties will be judged a classic in 20 years time, it would have to be the 1963 Studebaker Avanti. Indeed, it's already a "classic" in one sense, because it's still with us, albeit in a modified form.

The original Avanti was conceived largely by Sherwood Egbert, the hard-driving McCulloch executive who took over the president's chair in South Bend in 1960. Egbert thought a line of daringly different cars would help turn the ailing automaker around. He had already commissioned Brooks Stevens to update the Hawk and the Lark, and

decided to give Raymond Loewy a more interesting assignment. What Egbert wanted was a futuristic sports car that would lure people into Studebaker showrooms and inspire the next generation of Studebaker family cars.

Like most Studebaker projects in the early Sixties, the Avanti was a rush job carried out on an extremely tight budget. Loewy sequestered his design team (Robert F. Andrews, Frank Spring, Tom Kellogg, and John Ebstein) at his Palm Springs home, where they wouldn't be disturbed, and they finished a 1/8th-scale clay model in less

than a week. By April 1961, five weeks after the project had been initiated, a full-size clay had been completed and tooling orders were being placed.

The result was spectacular: long nose, "coke-bottle" waist, wraparound rear window, and bobbed rear deck. Some analysts decided there wasn't a straight line anywhere on it, but they might have missed the raised "gunsight" hood panel, placed asymmetrically on the left. The nose was bereft of grille (it was hidden below the blade-type front bumper), and this plus the smooth contours gave the

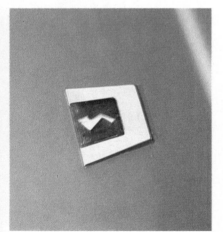

The name Avanti means "forward" in Italian, and the advanced design of this four-seat GT was totally unexpected from Studebaker. Some observers said there wasn't a straight line anywhere on the car, but the offset "gunsight" hood hump came as close as any. Cockpit design was aircraft-inspired, with a curved instrument cluster filled with clearly calibrated dials, toggle-style heater controls, an overhead console, and a safety-oriented padded rollover bar in the roof. Gas tank was placed behind the back seat for impact protection. (Owner: Bruce Williams)

behind the rear seat, an integral roll bar was molded into the roof, and doors closed on cone-type locks. Bendix front disc brakes provided excellent stopping power.

A credible GT needs a credible engine, and Studebaker worked miracles on its capable but old 289-cid

convertible frame was pressed into service. Fiberglass was chosen for the body to save tooling time and money, just as on the original Chevrolet Corvette. Safety was an important consideration in the Avanti design. The gas tank was put in a protected position in front of the trunk wall and

Avanti exceptionally good aerodynamics decades before car designers even thought about such considerations. Though this was an accident (Loewy had just guessed at the shape), it showed how "right" the design was. There was no money for a new chassis, so a heavily reinforced Lark

The 1963 Avanti's curvaceous lines are especially evident from the rear, and have stood the test of time exceptionally well. Styling was inspired by two earlier Loewy design exercises. (Owner: Bruce Williams)

V-8. The standard R1 version delivered an estimated 240 bhp, enough to keep the 3100-pound Avanti in the same league with garden-variety Corvettes. Then there was the supercharged R2. Developed by Andy Granatelli's Paxton Products, it made the car the performance equal of fuel-injected Corvettes and XK-E Jaguars. With the even hotter limited-production R3 and R4 units, Granatelli broke several stock car speed records at Bonneville in 1962 and again in '63.

Studebaker widely publicized the Avanti in the spring and summer of 1962, and the public's appetite was fully whetted. "Buff book" editors received preproduction models for test drives and all came away with very favorable impressions. Then disaster

struck. Molded Fiberglass Products of Ashtabula, Ohio, had been chosen to mold the fiberglass body, primarily because the company had experience building Corvette shells for Chevrolet. Unfortunately, the first 100 or so Avanti bodies were so poorly done as to be unuseable, which created a critical production delay. Says former Studebaker engineer Otto Klausmeyer: "The doors wouldn't close, the hoods were out of line, and the fender contours were mismatched." The Avanti finally arrived in dealer showrooms months after it had been expected, and it didn't sell. Controversy rages to this day as to whether the poor reaction was due to the delay, the high price ($4445), or Studebaker's "loser" image. In any event, only 3843 Avantis were built for '63. Another 809 were run off for 1964 before Studebaker beat a hasty retreat to Canada and ultimate extinction as an automaker. The brand-new 1963 Corvette Sting Ray provided stiff competition, but the Avanti's main

handicap was that it was a Studebaker. Two Studebaker dealers, Nate Altman and Leo Newman, refused to let the Avanti die when Studebaker left South Bend. After purchasing the production rights and some tooling, they formed the Avanti Motor Corporation, which produced a modified version with Corvette V-8 power called the Avanti II. These cars were largely hand-built customs, available with an almost unlimited choice of paints and interior trims—anything the customer wanted, in fact. The Avanti II continued through 1982, when the concern was purchased by construction tycoon Steven Blake. Today, his updated Avanti (minus the II designation) seems assured of a long and happy future.

Every Avanti is a collectible, due to low production and high status, but the ones with the Studebaker nameplate are most treasured by collectors today. After all, there's nothing quite like an original.